Six Buchan Villages
Re-visited

Dedicated to the memory of my father,
whose roots were in these parts, and written
especially for my grandchildren, James and Sophie

First published 2004 by
SCOTTISH CULTURAL PRESS
Unit 6, Newbattle Abbey Business Park
Newbattle Road, Dalkeith, EH22 3LJ, Scotland
Tel: +44 (0)131 660 6366 • Fax: +44 (0)131 660 4666
Email: info@scottishbooks.com
www.scottishbooks.com

Modern photographs © James Aitken; all others given to Margaret and
James Aitken by the people of the villages throughout the years
Cover photographs: *(front cover)* Boddam Castle;
(back cover) Buchan Ness Lighthouse, Boddam Harbour and Slains Castle

BRITISH LIBRARY CATALOGUING IN PUBLICATION DATA
A catalogue record for this book is available from the British Library

ISBN: 1 84017 051 4

Printed and bound by Bell & Bain Ltd, Glasgow

Six Buchan Villages
Re-visited

MARGARET AITKEN

SCOTTISH CULTURAL PRESS
www.scottishbooks.com

The Author

For the past 30 years Margaret Aitken and her husband have lived in Cruden Bay, Aberdeenshire. Her best-selling book, **In My Small Corner, Memories of an Orkney Childhood**, is also published by Scottish Cultural Press.

> 'I wish every ancestor of mine had done what
> Margaret Aitken has so beautifully done'
>
> *Review of In My Small Corner in*
> The Scots Magazine

Other books by the same author:

Six Buchan Villages

Twelve Light Years

In My Small Corner – Memories of an Orkney Childhood

Other North-East books by Scottish Cultural Press:

Aberdeens Around the World *Frederick Bull*

A Doric Dictionary *Douglas Kynoch*

Doric for Swots *Douglas Kynoch*

Doric Proverbs and Sayings *Douglas Kynoch (ed.)*

Huntly, Capital of Strathbogie *Cyril Barnes*

Moray Firth Ships & Trade *Ian Hustwick*

North East Song and Story *W. M. Wilson (ed.)*

Roots in a Northern Landscape *W.G. Lawrence*

Teach Yourself Doric *Douglas Kynoch*

Acknowledgements

I wish to thank:

Buchan Field Club for permission to quote from, and draw on articles by Miss Kathleen Macleod published in *Transactions of the Buchan Club.*

Mr Charlie Allan for permission to quote from *Farmer's Boy* and *The North East Lowlands of Scotland* by John R. Allan.

I especially want to acknowledge permission to freely use his book, *Slains and the Errolls* granted me by the late Sir Iain Moncreiffe of that Ilk.

I wish to thank the following for their help and assent to be interviewed:

Mrs Alison Allan, Oldcastle; Mr Burnett, Cruden Bay; Councillor S. Coull, Stirling Village; Mr Neil Davidson, Mintlaw; Mr Wm. Davidson, Peterhead; Mrs Forman, Maud; Mrs Elizabeth Hay, Collieston; Mr Tom Hay, ex-Whinnyfold; Dr L. Mackie, Collieston; Mr and Mrs J. Mathers, Cruden Bay; Mr and Mrs P. McClaughlan, Whinnyfold; Mrs McRobbie, Maud; Mrs Marian Morrison, Maud; Miss Betty May, Boddam; Mr A. Murison, Peterhead; Mr Jack Page, Collieston; Mr and Mrs Pinn, ex-Bullers o' Buchan; Mr R. Quinn, Cruden Bay; Rear Admiral S. Ritchie, Collieston; Mr Fergus Stephen, Longhaven; Mrs Veronica Smith, Bullers o' Buchan; Mr E. Taylor, Whinnyfold.

In addition, I would like to acknowledge the help given me in the 1970s by the following people, now sadly deceased:

Mrs Adams, Cruden Bay; Mrs Sally Bremner, Cruden Bay; Mr A. Buchan, Boddam; Mrs I. Buchan, Boddam; Mrs Buchan, Bullers o' Buchan; Mr Wm. Burnett, North Haven; Mr and Mrs Carmichael, Cruden Bay; Mr Joe Cay, Whinnyfold; Mrs Cruickshank, Cruden Bay; Mr Cruickshank, Cruden Bay; Lady Diana Hay, Countess of Erroll; Mr R. Ingram, Collieston; Mrs Lawson, Bullers o' Buchan; Mrs Philips, Cruden Bay; Mrs Philips, ex-Bullers o' Buchan; Mrs I. Robertson, ex-Bullers o' Buchan; Mrs Shearer, Cruden Bay; Mr and Mrs J. N. Stephen, Boddam; Mr Summers, Cruden Bay; Mrs Taylor, Whinnyfold.

Contents

Prologue

This is a story of castles and cottages. It tells the history of Boddam Castle, once owned by the Keiths of Ludquharn, and of Slains Castle, old and new. The present-day Slains Castle now stands on the cliff-tops to the north of the village of Cruden Bay, Aberdeenshire, and the remains of its predecessor, Old Slains Castle, can still be seen further south along the Buchan coast. Both were peopled by the great and ancient Scottish clan, the Hays of Erroll. Both are in ruins, and it is into those two gaunt shells that I shall try to breathe life by endeavouring to show the people who lived in them and tell of their doings.

The cottages I write of are those of the fishing villages in the neighbourhood of the castles. They are – Oldcastle, Cruden Bay, Bullers o' Buchan, Whinnyfold, Collieston and Boddam.

I first gathered together my findings on those castles and villages in the 1970s and presented these in a book entitled *Six Buchan Villages*. When *Six Buchan Villages* appeared, it was pointed out to me that I hadn't written about the farming community of the villages' hinterland. I now intend to rectify this, having studied the economic and cultural life of the farming folk of the countryside in the twentieth century.

This is one reason for bringing out another book based on a study of these villages.

Another is that *Six Buchan Villages* quickly sold out and is now out of print. Many people were disappointed when they could not obtain a copy, and a whole generation has grown up since 1976–77 when it was available.

None of the village people I interviewed in the 1970s are alive today. Therefore their conversations are now invaluable historical records and need to be preserved. This, to my mind, is the most important reason for my reiterating them in a more comprehensive work about this part of Buchan.

The following information, gleaned from many and various sources, consists of printed, published facts and information given to me by people of the villages and countryside. Nothing will be my invention. All will be as true as the sources of the facts allow. I cannot vouch for the veracity of the writers who recorded their stories but, unless I am very much mistaken, I am sure that the villagers and people of the countryside who spoke to me of their past were as truthful as memory allows any of us to be.

CHAPTER ONE

Oldcastle

There's a rough cart-track about 17 miles to the north-east of Aberdeen that peeters out beside an A-frame cottage perched on a rocky promontory in the shadow of a dark, ruined castle.

Lady Diana Hay, the late Countess of Erroll, raised the A-frame house from the remains of one or two cottages when, as late as 1950, she regained a small area of land at Oldcastle that had once been part of her ancestor's extensive estates.

In 1594, James VI discovered that her ancestor, Francis 9th Earl of Erroll, together with two other Roman Catholic noblemen, had sent the King of Spain a signed blank treaty to obtain that monarch's assistance to persuade James VI to adopt their faith, depose Elizabeth from the English throne, and replace her with their converted king. At news of this, James VI sent an army against them. They defeated it, whereupon James rode north himself. Sir Iain Moncreiffe in his book *Slains and the Errolls* explains that 'the Earls were too loyal to his person to resist,' and fled abroad. The king proceeded to destroy their homes. He himself rode out from Aberdeen to personally superintend the blowing up of Old Slains Castle.

The Kingis Majestie come to Aberdein with his armie, about the xv day of October 1594. The houssis of Straboggie and Slaynis, with the Newtoun, a gallant house, wer distroyed and dimolyshit, and the King rod theare to that effect in propper persone.

So it was that Francis 9th Earl of Erroll, returned from three years in exile to find his stout castle reduced to the rickle of stones that still overshadows Lady Diana's house.

The Countess of Erroll did not flee with her husband nor did she follow him into exile. When her home was demolished she moved into the farmhouse of Clochtow about half a mile from Old Slains Castle. There she stayed and, even when Francis returned and his estates were restored to him, she preferred to be known as the 'Guidwife of Clochtow' rather than Lady Erroll. It was some time before she left the farmhouse.

Between the castle ruins and the Countess's A-frame house, a battered old cannon points out to sea. This relic was, according to Sir Iain Moncreiffe, raised from the Spanish galleon, *Santa Catarina*, which had been wrecked in the bay beside the castle as she brought arms and treasure for the Earls' rebellion. Another school of thought believes that the sunken ship belonged to the Spanish Armada, defeated six years before the Earls' revolt. Whatever the truth, the bay was ever after called 'St Catherine's Dub'.

Carved on the wall of the house is a falcon – the crest of the Hays of Erroll – and beside the front door is a smooth, grey boulder known as the 'Hech Heigh Stane'. Above the fireplace in the Countess's sitting room there is a stone slab on which are carved two ploughmen with their plough yokes. So did the late Countess commemorate the legendary beginnings of her family.

The legend so illustrated was alleged to have its source at the Battle of Luncarty between Scots and Danes in 980 in Perthshire. The only escape route from the battle-field was via a narrow pass and through it the defeated Scots were fleeing when three nearby ploughmen decided to take part in the action. The three were an old man and his two sons, and armed with what implements they had to hand – the father bearing the yoke that connected his two oxen to the plough – they took up positions in the narrow pass and killed each would-be escapee, Scot or Dane. This forced the Scots to turn again and face the foe, who, surprised by the renewed attack, were soundly defeated. The grateful Scottish king summoned the three ploughmen heroes and announced that as a reward for their courageous successful intervention they could have as much land in the Carse of Gowrie as a hound would run

The 'Hech Heigh Stane'

over or as a falcon would pass over in flight. The old man decided that he would accept the land flown over by the falcon. This area consisted of the lands of Erroll by the Tay in Perthshire marked at their boundaries by ancient stones – one of which came eventually to the Erroll estate in Buchan, Aberdeenshire.

A story arose about this stone. It was supposed to be the one on which the old ploughman had sat to recover from his exertions after turning the tide of battle. Sitting there, he sighed wearily, 'Hech, Heigh,' whereupon the King said, 'Hech, heigh, say ye, and Hay shall ye be!' so giving the owners of the lands of Erroll their surname: Hay. The story survives despite evidence to the fact that surnames were not in existence in Scotland at the early date given for this incident.

However, when heraldry arrived many centuries later, three red escutcheons said to represent the three ploughmen appeared on the Erroll family's silver shield. It has been suggested that this was a 'fanciful' interpretation of the arms which were first displayed on the seal of David Hay, 2nd Baron of Erroll, (1195–1230). Then, at the end of the Middle Ages, the Errolls changed their crest a third time. It had been a stag's head, then it was a bull's or ox's head, and now it became

The arms of the Hays of Erroll, set above
the late Countess's fireplace in Oldcastle

a falcon in memory of the legend. For a badge they decided on an ox-yoke supported by two laurel entwined ploughmen holding ox-yokes. As long as the Hays of Erroll have had a motto it has been – 'Serva Jugum' which translated is 'Preserve the Yoke'.

History records that the first appearance of the Hay family name in Scotland was about 1160 with William de la Haye, or 'William of the Wooden Castle', as Sir Iain Moncreiffe told me, and not 'of the Golden Castle or Palisade' as misprinted in his book *Slains and the Errolls* when reprinted in Peterhead. This William was cup-bearer to King Malcolm. About ten years passed and King William I ('William the Lion') gave William Hay a charter conferring upon him the Barony of Erroll with the proviso that, in time of war, he would send 'two knights fully armed, mounted, equipped and rationed, together with their due retinue of esquires, men-at-arms and archers to fight for the king. William, now 1st Baron of Erroll, was also William the Lion's cup-bearer. When William the Lion was taken prisoner at Alnwick in 1174 one of the conditions for his release in the Treaty of Falaise was that several of his Scottish nobles were to be taken hostage by the English. William, 1st Baron of Erroll, was one of them.

William married Eva and their son, David Hay, 2nd Baron of Erroll, married Ethna whose father was Gilbert, the Celtic Earl of Strathearn. So the name Gilbert came into the Hay family and appears several times in their family tree.

Indeed, the third baron was named Gilbert and he became one of the Regents of Scotland during the childhoods of Alexander II in 1225 and Alexander III in 1258. Gilbert Hay married Lady Idonea Comyn whose father was the Earl of Buchan and whose brother was Constable of Scotland. Sir Iain Moncreiffe points out that this marriage 'first brought the Errolls in contact with the Great Office of Constable, which they still hold, and brought also to them the blood of the ancient Celtic rulers of Buchan since prehistoric times – the semi-royal line of Bede the Pict'.

The next of the Erroll line to make a name in Scottish history was Sir Gilbert Hay, 5th Baron of Erroll who allied himself with Robert Bruce, and accompanied him in all the vicissitudes he endured in his struggle for the Scottish crown. Sir Gilbert is believed to have borne the mace at Bruce's coronation at Scone, and when Gilbert's cousins, the Comyns, were bereft of their lands of Slains in Buchan by Bruce, those lands and the Comyns' Office of Constable were passed over to the Hays of Erroll. Sir Iain Moncreiffe explains the role of Constable:

The Constable was the commander-in-chief, under the King of the feudal Army – the guardian of the King's person and dwelling – the supreme judge in all criminal matters within four miles of the King, called the Verge – the Protector of the Parliament House – and the umpire in tournaments and Ordeals by combat. The Constable comes next to the Royal family and has precedence before every other hereditary honour.

When Parliament was sitting, the High Constable rode on the King's right hand carrying a white baton to show he was in command, and sat on the King's right hand separate from the other nobles and with the honours laid in front of him.

After Bruce's victory at Bannockburn Sir Gilbert became his Ambassador who arranged the peace terms with the defeated Edward II of England.

Sir Gilbert's grandson, Sir David Hay, 6th Baron of Erroll, died in 1346 at the Battle of Neville's Cross where King David Bruce was captured by the English.

Sir Thomas, the 7th Baron of Erroll, married King Robert II's daughter, Princess Elizabeth, whose sister became one of our Queen's ancestors by her marriage with Sir John Lyon of Glamis.

The year 1449 brought more honours to the Hays of Erroll. Sir William, 9th Baron of Erroll, became Lord Hay, and three years later became Earl of Erroll and Lord Glamis. He married Beatrice, a sister of the last 'Black' Earl of Douglas.

Sir William's grandson, another William, 4th Earl of Erroll and Hereditary Sheriff of Aberdeen, died fighting for and beside King James IV on Flodden Field. Besides the Earl, 87 gentlemen of the Hay Clan fell that day and with them many of their men.

The direct line of males to hold the title Earl of Erroll failed with the death at the age of twenty of William's great-grandson, yet another William Hay. This William's place was taken by a cousin, George, who became 7th Earl of Erroll. George's son, Andrew, married Lady Jane Hay, sister of his deceased cousin, and so the two branches of the family were joined in the person of his son, Francis, 9th Earl of Erroll.

Francis was not allowed to become heir apparent without trouble. The Earl's eldest son was deaf and dumb, and two of the Earl's brothers opposed the succession of the younger Francis. One dark night they, with armed followers and helped by other relatives in the castle, scaled the outer walls of the stronghold, captured the Earl, threw him in the dungeon tower and kept him there for a month. Fortunately, King James VI himself took a hand in the proceedings. He had Parliament pass a special Act which ensured that Francis would become the next Earl of Erroll. As a further precaution, Francis, now the new Master of Erroll, was placed in the care of the Keeper of Edinburgh Castle. Sir Iain Moncreiffe states in *Slains and the Errolls*:

> At this time Old Slains Castle was almost the centre of a little principality. The Earls of Erroll had powers of life and death nor did the authority of the ordinary Law Courts extend into the Regality and Lordship of Slains.

It's amazing, when looking at the tottering ruin, to think that ladies-in-waiting and page-boys once trotted about busily within those walls. That ladies peeped from its windows at hawking and hunting parties riding out for their sport. One such lady, in an earlier era when the Tower of Buchan, as it was then known, belonged to the family of Comyn, was Isabella, Countess of Buchan, who placed the crown of Scotland on Bruce's head. For this she was displayed in a cage-like room at Berwick Castle for a number of years on the orders of a furious Edward I.

On fine, bracing days, the Chamberlain, Baillie, Secretary, Steward, Standard Bearer, Marischal, Master of the Horse, Chaplain, esquires, grooms of the chamber and men-at-arms possibly congregated on the flat piece of ground above the castle – still called the Tilting Ground –

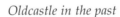

Oldcastle in the past

and held tournaments. On dark nights when the sea raged and beat against the rocky promontory, and the wind howled around the bleak walls, there were banquets – music filled the halls, the Jester entertained, the noble inmates amused themselves with games of chess, draughts and backgammon or listened while stirring stories were read to them.

It's quite probable that round this stronghold of the great and powerful there were humble hovels, housing men who caught fish for the Earl's table, and women who gathered 'buckies' (whelks) from the rocks to add to m'lady's delicacies.

Thanks to Earl Francis, however, Old Slains Castle was blasted out of existence. After he was allowed to return, Earl Francis and his household, in which there was now a French valet called Beaugre, took themselves off to the cliff-tops above Cruden Bay and built a new Slains Castle. It was believed that Earl Francis had a secret passage tunnelled out beneath his new castle, the passageway leading out on to land which he gave to Beaugre, who called it after his native Fontainebleau. The farm retains its name to this day and there are still descendants of the valet, who are now called Beagrie or Bagrie, in the area. Often in this family the Christian name, Frank (after Earl Francis), appears.

Whether ordinary folk just continued to struggle to exist beside the old castle or simply moved in and settled when the Earl moved out – probably utilising the stones of the collapsed castle to build houses – is not known, but by 1791 there was a village called Oldcastle on the site. In 1840 there were 14 houses and 48 inhabitants who, with the people of the next village of Collieston, were described as being 'superior to other working tradesmen in the property which they possess, never interfere in the politics of the day, and are most regular attendants on the public ordinances of religion.'

In 1855, there were three 18ft to 30ft boats and three under 18ft there. Fishermen and boys numbered 18; gutters and packers, 18; and vendors, makers of nets, etc., 25. In 1881, there were 21 boats and 42 fishermen.

In March 1900, gale-force winds whipped up raging seas round Oldcastle, destroying boats and fishing equipment to such an extent

Oldcastle as it was in the 1970s

that the last nine families – 60 members of the speedily depopulating village – up and left for Aberdeen.

The gale was simply a final straw. As early as 1883 one fisherman from the village had joined a deputation to London to ask Mr Chamberlain to take some action to prevent the marauding trawlers from taking away the livelihood of the fishing villages. The minister gave the delegates no encouragement.

Not surprisingly, by the winter of 1900 a day's fishing would quite frequently result in a catch of two to four haddocks. When they did catch marketable amounts of fish, women had to carry them four miles to the nearest railway station. The railway and salesmen then took their share of the meagre profits. Sometimes a cwt. of haddocks earned as little as 7/- sometimes less. They must have been hard put to find the 25/- annual rent charged by the proprietrix, Lady Gordon Cathcart.

Mr J. Philips in Cruden Bay, whom I discovered to be a nephew of Miss Margaret Philips, the last old lady reluctantly to join the trek from the village to Aberdeen, agreed that life at Oldcastle had been hard. He recalled that his mother used to walk over the links to an ice-house in Newburgh – a distance of about four miles – with salmon in her creel, returning laden with coal. He remembered too how the folk used to collect the 'buckies' – whelks – to sell for a pittance per peck in Aberdeen.

It would seem that some of the 'trekkers' did not care for city life, for in 1928 a newspaper correspondent found three cottages inhabited. One tenant was 'a bearded old salt' constantly scanning the horizon with his 'spy-glasses'; he had given up fishing. One was an elderly woman, and the other was a young man in his thirties working the sole boat, but looking forward to being joined the next year by a friend and his boat. This reporter states 'in the thriving days of the village 12 boats carried on a successful fishing.'

In 1929, Peter Anson wrote 'most of the cottages had been abandoned and were little more than heaps of stones,' but he noticed two boats drawn up on the shore —'the property of the little remnant who still carry on fishing, from this, perhaps the most curiously situated fishing village on the east coast of Scotland.'

Mrs Elizabeth Hay used to visit Oldcastle in the 1950s. She told me that at that time, in one of the cottages that was to become the Countess of Erroll's A-frame house, there was a woman resident; that a cottage known as Dickson's was occupied; and that Mr John Sutherland, whom she visited, lived in another cottage, now a ruin. Mr Sutherland grew vegetables in his garden to which many migratory birds, such as gold-crested wrens, came to rest. Mr Sutherland was very interested in birds and very knowledgeable about them. It would seem that he did not frequently leave his cottage. Mrs Hay said the postman was a link between him and the outside world, bringing some essentials as well as mail which he left at the farm just above Oldcastle. Other supplies were brought as far as the farm by vans. Mrs Hay remembered a baker's van and that of a general merchant. She also recalled going down the steep path with her bucket to the North Bay where the vital well supplied water for the village. She remembered that the water was procured through a tap at that time.

When I visited Oldcastle in the 1970s only the Countess's house was occupied, and her tenants were resurrecting three old cottage remains to make another modern residence. The new residence is now complete. It is called Dickson's Cottage. From David Toulmin's book,

Travels without a Donkey, I see that Mr Martin Dickson, after whom presumably the cottage is named, was a publisher who worked under the name of Michael Slains.

Besides the late Countess's house and Dickson's Cottage there are Potter's Cottage, which used to be called 'Hame', and Morrison's Cottage. Mr and Mrs John Allan live in Morrison's Cottage. Mrs Allan kindly invited me in and made coffee. Instead of having coffee, I asked her for a glass of water from the all important well, now equipped with an electric pump. I asked about social life in Oldcastle. It seemed to be a friendly community of professional people who enjoy the social activities of the much bigger neighbouring village of Collieston.

Thinking over our pleasant visit, I realised I had unwittingly tasted the same water sipped by the brave Countess of Buchan all those centuries ago. The past entwines the present at Oldcastle.

CHAPTER TWO

Cruden Bay

THE ERROLLS OF SLAINS CASTLE

The tenants of the Erroll estates laughed and applauded when the eldest son of the family – Lord Kilmarnock – declared in a speech – 'I consider myself to be uncommonly fortunate to have attained my majority in the glorious year in which our most gracious Sovereign has celebrated her Diamond Jubilee, and which, moreover, has witnessed the almost equally important event of the opening of the Cruden Railway.'

The year was 1897, and the occasion was a dinner given on the clifftops to the north of Cruden Bay on 24 October for the Erroll estate's tenant farmers, almost one hundred guests, as part of the week's celebrations to mark the coming of age of the heir to Slains Castle.

The West Hall of the castle was decorated throughout with evergreens. Behind the chairman was the Erroll family's motto – 'The Hays shall flourish and their good grey hawk shall nocht flinch before the blast.' This had been formed out of evergreens and art muslin, and, at either side of the motto was 'K' for Kilmarnock and 'E' for Erroll in gold. On the entrance door at the other end of the hall was a sign saying 'Welcome' and over an ornamental arch inside the hall was 'K' for Kilmarnock, 'October 17th 1897' – Lord Kilmarnock's birthday. Round the walls, embedded among the evergreens were copies of the family crest, a falcon, and in a large recess was displayed the arms of the Earls of Erroll, which consisted of a shield flanked on either side by a ploughman bearing a yoke.

The falcon on the home of the late Countess of Erroll

The company had dined well. The menu read:

Soups Hare Soup, Scotch Broth **Fish** Turbot, Lobster Sauce, Baked Stuffed Haddock **Roasts** Corned Beef, Roast Beef, Roast Lamb, Marbled Goose **Puddings** Plum Pudding **Sweets** Apple Tart, Kilmarnock Pudding, Jellies, Creams, Prunes, Figs **Dessert**

The Errolls and their tenants seem to have always valued the family's legendary beginnings. On the occasion in 1897, described above, and on other reported celebrations, the castle was decorated in a very similar way, in remembrance of the story that has been passed down through generations.

Up till the time of Francis, 9th Earl of Erroll, the Erroll family home, as we have seen, was the Old Castle of Slains. It was Francis who is credited with at least starting the building of Slains Castle in 1597 on his return from exile in France and it was he who set up house in Slains Castle on Bowness north of Cruden Bay.

Earl Francis married three times. His first wife was Lady Anne Stuart, daughter of the Earl of Atholl; his second was Lady Margaret Stuart, daughter of the Regent Moray, natural brother of Mary, Queen of Scots. Then Earl Francis fell in love, much to the displeasure of King James VI, with Lady Elizabeth Douglas. This lady was one of seven beautiful sisters, daughters of the 7th Earl of Morton, and known as the 'Seven Pearls of Lochleven'. Against the king's wishes, Earl Francis married Lady Elizabeth.

Earl Francis did not enjoy uninterrupted domestic bliss with all three wives. The second one, Lady Margaret, fell out with him to the extent of presenting him with a list of domestic utensils which she proposed taking with her on leaving him. This list gives us some idea of how the castle's rooms were equipped at that time.

The geir within Slains, as following quhilk my Lady desyris –
Item of fedder beddis, xxx; Item of bowsteris, xxix; Item of pewter pleittis, viij; Item of truncheouris, xxviij; Item of spittis, iiij; Item of raxis, ij; Item of pottis of brass and yring, xv; Item of panis, viiij; Item of barrelis within the Place, xxxviij; heirof xxxiij barrelis for aill; item of tyne quart stoppis, iiij; with ane choppin stope; Item of chandelleris, xj; heirof twa of trine; Item, twa morteris with their pestollis.

The Earl was having none of it. He endorsed the document:

To my ladyse gredie and vnressonable desyris it is answerit. That seeing the haill plenissing found in the House of Logie and the outvyle of the plenissing left be hir in Slanis is all ower littill to pleneiss ane of the Places. My Lord can spair na pairt theirof.

Earl Francis also had a spirited stepmother, Lady Agnes Sinclair. In 1601 this Countess of Erroll cocked a snook at the reformed Church. The Church insisted that Midsummer Eve be held as a Fast Day. Lady Agnes celebrated it by following the Roman Catholic custom of lighting bonfires. She positioned her 'bleezis of fire' in the vicinity of the minister's house.

The next and 10th Earl, William, in his position of High Constable of Scotland, attended Charles I's coronation. However, it was as a result of his extravagant lifestyle that the Erroll lands in Perthshire had to be sold.

Earl Francis' grandson, Gilbert, 11th Earl of Erroll, was married to Lady Katherine Carnegie who, according to a bawdy ballad, accused her husband of being impotent. This charge he proved untrue when, in front of 'wise judges' he demonstrated he was a man with a 'willing servant maid.' But he left no descendant to carry on the Erroll line. Gilbert made so many additions to the Castle that he came to be regarded as its founder and much of the present ruins date from his time.

We have some idea of how Earl Gilbert spent his money from the following extract found in *Turreff's Antiquarian Gleanings from Aberdeenshire Records*. It contains an account of the Earl of Errol's expenditure upon his way to Scone, where he was to officiate as Lord High Constable at the Coronation of King Charles the Second:

Extracts from a Household Book of the Family of Errol,
kept from the Year 1650 to 1660
Dischairg beginning the 24th Dec. 1650

Dec. 24	Item, for a grit bitt to yur Lordship pownie,	£0	13	4
	Item to Jas. Morrison, Cordiner, at Peterhead,			
	for a pair of blak walking boots to yur Lo:	12	0	0
	Item, to him for a pair of shoes to your Lo: at	3	0	0
	Item, to his son in drink-money	0	18	0
Dec. 25	To William Fraser in Kintore for supper and			
	breakfast, and for corne and stra one night,			
	according to his bill,	10	6	4
	Item, to his servants,	0	18	0
Dec. 27	Item, given to my Lord Fraser's servants,			
	at Muchalls, your Lo: being there one night,	8	5	0
	Item, to the stable groom there,	1	10	10
	Item, to Kinmundies's man when he brought			
	his master's horse to your Lo:	0	12	0

	Item, for supper and breakfast at Fettercairn, in Harie Blafouris,			
	Item, for corne and stra for 7 horses one night there,			
	Item, to the servants in drink-money,			
Dec. 29	Item, to the kirk box at Forfar,	£0	12	0
	Item, to the beddal there,	0	12	0
	Item, to the poor there,	0	6	0
Dec. 30	Item, to the servants at Brigton, your Lo: being there two nights,	5	8	0
	Item, for aill at Forfar between sermons,	0	10	0
	Item for fraught of horse and men at Perth,	1	4	0
	Item, to a pint of aill to James McKinge, that was sent before,	0	2	0
	Item, for 8 whyte battons to your Lo: and friends at the coronacioun,	5	8	0
	Item, that day for fraught of horse and men to Scoone and from it	0	18	0
	Item for seck, sugar, and aill, in your Lo: chamber the first night,	1	6	0
1651				
Jan. 2	Item, given to his Majestie's footmen,	8	14	0
	Item, to 5 of his Majestie's trumpeters,	12	0	0
	Item, to his Majestie's coachman,	2	18	0
	Item, to blind Edward the songster,	0	12	0
Jan. 5	Item, to the poor,	0	6	0
Jan. 7	Item, to a poor boy,	0	2	0
	Item, for bread and aill the night that Roxb; and Erskin suppit with your Lo:	1	6	0
	Item, for fleshes frae Effie Murray's that night, conform to her bill,	9	12	0
	Item, to John Mackrath, barbar, for trimming your Lo: 3 times at Perth,	6	8	0
Jan. 13	Item, to the man that helpit on with your Lo: robes at Perth and Scoone,	0	12	0
	Item, to Andro Kid, Merchant at Perth, according to his subjoinct accompts,	552	0	0
	Item, to the kirk box at Perth	0	12	0

	Item, to Peter Littlejohn, tailyour conferz to his accompt at Perth,	£55	1	0
	Item, to him to pay Walter Younge, for ane gold hat-band, wying twa uns and 10 drops, at 10 pound the uns gude,	27	10	0
	Item, to your Lo: dyet for several times at Effie Murray's and David Jack's, paid by Alex. Hay,	10	13	0
	Item, to a Minstrel at Effie Murray's, at your Lo; direction	1	4	0
	Item, to the poor that day,	0	7	0
	Item, for bread and drink at your Lo: collacioun ane morning the time your Lo: was at Perth,	2	7	4
	Item, given at your Lo: direction to Edward the fooll,	2	18	0
	Item, to a blind man at Brigton,	0	6	0
	Item, to the poor at Forfar	0	6	0
Jan. 16	Item, for supper and breakfast at Brechin,	7	6	0
	Item, in drink-money to the servants,	1	4	0
	Item, to a boy for his help at brig of Leipie	0	3	4
Jan. 17	Item, for supper, breakfast, and seck, at Drum Leithie ane night,	12	16	0
	Item, for corne and stra to 7 horse there,	4	8	0
	Item, for a shoe to the black pownie	0	5	0
	Item, to the servants there,	0	18	0
	Item, to the poor there,	0	6	0
	Item, for supper + breakfast at Susanna Hayes,	11	2	0
	Item, to the servants there,	1	4	0
	Item, to the poor at Foveran,	0	6	0
	Item, to Robert Hay, boatman,	0	12	0
Jan. 19	Item, to the kirk box at Cruden,	0	12	0
Jan. 20	Item, to a post with a Letter to Crimonmogate,	0	6	0
Jan. 22	Item to Kinmundies's man when he took back his master's horse your Lo: had south	1	10	0

Because Earl Gilbert had taken part in Charles II's coronation at Scone in 1651, he was, some time later, fined £2,000 by Cromwell. However when the Restoration eventually came he was made a Privy Councillor.

Earl Gilbert's wife, Lady Katherine, was a staunch supporter of the Jacobite cause and having been caught smuggling letters and money to help Graham of Claverhouse, or 'Bonnie Dundee', was imprisoned in Edinburgh Castle. Somehow she made her escape and fled to the Jacobite Court of St Germain in France where she became Lady Chief Governess to the boy who grew up to be the 'Old Chevalier'. She lived there the rest of her life.

Sir John Hay, from another branch of the family, succeeded Gilbert and became 12th Earl. He was also married to an enthusiast for Jacobitism, Lady Anne Drummond. Her brothers, the Duke of Perth and the Duke of Melfort, ruled Scotland under James VII, and accompanied him into exile. Lady Anne carried on a secret correspondence with her brothers and other leading Jacobites, writing her letters in milk or code.

Lady Anne also held court for her Jacobite allies in her Holyrood apartment in Edinburgh. They came not only to gossip with her, but to ask her opinion on Scottish affairs. She must have felt she was in charge of Scotland. When Claverhouse amazed everybody by marrying a woman from the enemy Covenanter camp, he not only had to face the opposition and mockery of his Jacobite associates, many of whom considered him a backslider, but there was also Lady Erroll's displeasure to be endured.

It was in Lady Anne's time too that Episcopalianism was being forcibly replaced by Presbyterianism. When her relative, Dr James Drummond, Bishop of Brechin, was deprived of his see, she invited him to make Slains Castle his home.

On 19 September, 1688, a gentleman, J. Hay, wrote to Lady Anne from Edinburgh. He had news, no doubt of great interest to her, of preparations being made to repel an expected invasion by William of Orange.

The letter ended on more mundane matters: 'I caused my wyfe buy the satin and flannen your ladyship ordered which James Body is to send by the bearer. They are the best of both she could get.' So life in Slains Castle wasn't all codes and intrigues!

This same J. Hay also wrote to Lady Anne about her eldest daughter, Lady Mary Hay, who, in 1693, was benefiting greatly from 'tyme she has been at schooles in Edinburgh'.

Lady Anne's and Sir John's son, Charles, who became 13th Earl of Erroll, felt very strongly that Scotland and England should not unite in 1707. In 1708, he made various alterations to the castle, including giving it a new front, but perhaps more importantly he was visited by a secret agent sent by the Old Pretender with a signed and sealed order. This missive ordered the Earl to send a pilot to meet the French fleet off Fifeness and guide the would-be king's ship up the River Forth. Unfortunately for the Jacobite side, the pilot duly engaged got drunk and failed to meet the French, and a squadron of English ships arrived on the scene and drove James and the French back to France. Immediately afterwards Charles, Earl of Erroll, was arrested and imprisoned in Edinburgh Castle where, in a quarrel with the Earl Marischal who was also a Jacobite prisoner, he threw a bottle at the latter which wounded him in the head. It's only fair to note that Earl Charles was not in the best of health at the time.

Charles was unmarried and the last male in his line. Consequently, he was succeeded in 1717 by his sister, Lady Mary, who became 14th in the line of Earls of Erroll.

Politically, the Countess Mary followed in her mother's footsteps. She recruited from the Buchan area as many soldiers as she could to fight for Charles Edward Stuart at Culloden. After that defeat, many of her Jacobite friends lay in hiding throughout the countryside. Lady Mary kept in touch with them, employing as her messenger Jamie Fleeman, the Laird of Udny's fool – an apparently simple-minded fellow.

The Countess used to ride to Aberdeen preceded by Jamie riding on a stick. When they came to the River Ythan Jamie would turn to face her and ford the river backwards, shouting to her from time to time: 'Ye've nae got afore me yet, your ladyship, I think,' and laughing uproariously at his joke. Lady Mary had a drawing of Jamie hung in the drawing room of Slains Castle. This drawing had been made surreptitiously as Jamie sat in a tavern unaware of the artist who was a friend of the Countess. The artist seized the opportunity, though not equipped with drawing materials, and drew Jamie's likeness with a burnt stick on pasteboard. Lady Mary begged this, the only known likeness of Jamie, from her friend.

Lady Mary married Alexander Falconer, who took the name of Hay on his marriage. They were buried side by side in the aisle of St Ternan's Church, Collieston, and from the inscription on their tombstone we can gather that Lady Mary's marriage was a happy one.

'Under this tombstone are laid, not gold or silver nor treasures of any kind, but the bodies of a most affectionate pair, Mary, Countess of Errol and Alexander Hay of Delgaty, who lived in wedlock peacefully and lovingly for twenty seven years, and who desired to be buried side by side . . . '

Lady Mary had no children so was succeeded by James, Lord Boyd, grandson of her sister, Lady Margaret Hay, and son of Lady Anne Livingston, Margaret's daughter, whose husband was the Earl of Kilmarnock. James became 15th Earl of Erroll and the last Earl of Kilmarnock.

This Earl held a place of importance at the coronation of George III in 1761, and was escort to George's bride-to-be, Princess Charlotte of Mecklenburg, on her journey to England. At the coronation, Earl James was described as 'the most magnificent figure'. He forgot to remove his hat but, as he started to apologise, King George insisted that the hat remain on his head 'for he looked on his presence at the solemnity as a very particular honour'. Sir Iain Moncreiffe makes the point that, 'He was in fact the first Hay to act in person as Lord High Constable of Scotland at the coronation of a Hanoverian King.' Unhappily, in order to accommodate George III's wish that he be sent to escort Princess Charlotte, the Earl had to sell the town of Turriff, a family possession since 1412, and the castle of Delgaty to defray his expenses on this mission.

This was the Earl who one evening in 1773, came home to find two notable visitors awaiting his return. Countess Isabella, his second wife, was entertaining Dr Johnson and James Boswell who had arrived at Slains Castle as the bell was ringing for dinner at three o'clock.

After the meal, Lady Isabella lined up eight of her children for her guests' inspection. A baby girl was excluded. Lady Erroll's brother-in-law, Charles Boyd, was also present, and, after the introduction of the children (and presumably after they and their mother had withdrawn), he told the guests 'that Lady Errol was one of the most pious and sensible women in the island, had a good head, and as good a heart . . . she did not use force or fear in educating her children.' Whereupon, Dr Johnson announced, 'Sir, she is wrong.' Seemingly, Lady Erroll's method of upbringing was one of 'exciting emulation' and 'making comparisons of superiority,' amongst the children. Johnson thought a whack with the rod was preferable, as Lady Erroll's technique would 'make brothers and sisters hate each other'.

Dr Johnson was, however, favourably impressed by the castle:

We came in the afternoon to *Slanes Castle*, built upon the margin of the sea, so that the walls of one of the towers seem only a continuation of a perpendicular rock, the foot of which is beaten by the waves. To walk round the house seemed impractable. From the windows the eye wanders over the sea that separates Scotland from Norway, and when the winds beat with violence must enjoy all the terrifick grandeur of the tempestuous ocean. I would not for my amusement wish for a storm; but as storms, whether wished or not, will sometimes happen, happen, I may say, without violation of humanity, that I should willingly look out upon them from Slanes Castle.

James Boswell paid heed to the castle's landward environment, and commented that, 'though from its being just on the North-east Ocean, no trees will grow here, Lord Errol has done all that can be done. He has cultivated his fields so as to bear rich crops of every kind, and he has made an excellent kitchen-garden, with a hot-house.'

When, after dinner, Dr Johnson proposed their departure, Mr Boyd pressed them to stay overnight and so meet his brother who would return in the evening. Lady Erroll, who had left the room previously, sent for Charles Boyd, and on hearing of the famous pair's intention to leave, sent him back with the message that she would never let Dr Johnson into the house again if he went away that night. She had made plans for her guests' further entertainment, having ordered the coach to take them to see two natural phenomena of the district – Dun Buy rock and the Bullers o' Buchan.

The next Earl was George, 16th in line, who shot himself in 1798 having by mistake let out a secret with which he had been entrusted by the Prime Minister, Mr Pitt. George was followed by his brother, William Hay, who became 17th Earl of Erroll. William, like his father and brother, was not a wise manager. When he died, the Errolls' lands had been reduced by 12 estates. William's eldest son, James, was killed at the battle of Quatre Bras in 1815, one of the battles connected to Wellington's victory at Waterloo. This meant that William was succeeded by his second son, William George, 18th Earl of Erroll.

Nothing is known of the Countess Elizabeth, wife of George, 16th Earl of Erroll, nor about Jane, Alicia and Harriet, the three wives of William 17th Earl, but William George, the 18th Earl, made a link with royalty by his marriage. His bride was Lady Elizabeth Fitzclarence, daughter of William IV and the actress, Mrs Jordan. She is pictured in a portrait of the Fitzclarence family which hangs in House of Dun near Montrose. This Countess kept, as mementoes, the stone thrown by a mad sailor at her father at Ascot and the gloves King William wore when he first opened Parliament.

William George was made a peer of the United Kingdom and was given the title of Baron Kilmarnock in 1841. More honours followed, including the position of High Marischal of Scotland and High Steward of William IV's Household. This was the Earl who completely rebuilt the castle in 1836–37.

His son, William Harry, who became 19th Earl of Erroll in 1846, married Eliza Amelia Gore. Lady Eliza accompanied her husband to the Crimean War. Since he had to fight, he slept in the camp bed and she slept on the ground. When she passed through Constantinople the Sultan presented her with a white horse which she named Sultan after him.

Lady Eliza was one of Queen Victoria's ladies-in-waiting. The Queen became godmother to the Countess's grandson – called Victor after the Queen. In her capacity as lady-in-waiting, the Countess was present at the first royal christening in Scotland for 300 years. The baby christened was the daughter of Princess Beatrice and Prince Henry of

*Painting of Lady Erroll and Sultan, the white horse given to
her during the Crimean War by the Sultan of Turkey
(by kind permission of the late Countess of Erroll)*

Battenberg. This event took place in a tartan upholstered drawing
room in Balmoral Castle. Evergreens, palms and ferns decorated the
room while the baptismal font, containing water from the River Jordan,
was wreathed in jasmine and white lilies.

Sir Iain Moncreiffe had a considerable amount of information about
William Harry. He described him as 'a hot tempered but generous
eccentric'. Every morning Earl Harry started the day with a cold, seawater bath. His Fool, whose name was Sandy Summers, but known to
the locals as 'Sandy Sheep', pumped up the water for Earl Harry into a
bathroom in the stout, square tower that rises from the sea. Sometimes
the bath did not fill no matter how diligently poor Sandy pumped.
Some of the other servants had removed the plug as a rather cruel trick.

Painting of Harry, 19th Earl of Erroll (by kind permission of the late Countess of Erroll)

Usually Earl Harry wore a 'tweed suit and a high Glengarry bonnet' with the falcon of the Hays' crest in silver pinned on it. Then the Earl with his large dog would visit his fishing village of Port Erroll where he expected every male to doff his cap and every female to curtsey. Apart from this insistence, he behaved humanely and generously to the fisher community. He would not permit a public house or poorhouse on his estate, but if people were in dire straits he gave no money but food produced on his home farm and gardens and 'chits on particular shops ordering them to be supplied with articles of clothing on his account'. He had a football pitch and cricket ground made, and gave all the equipment needed to play those games in which his sons played leading parts. He had built a reading room and 'kept a fire there all winter'. In the reading room he had dominoes supplied, but the playing of cards he forbade. When the villagers wanted a Congregational Church in the village he gave money and land for its building. His wife and daughters taught in its Sunday School. When he attended the Presbyterian Church, a mile or so out of the village, he was famed for showing his impatience with what he considered to be over lengthy sermons by lowering 'his watch on its gold chain over the side of his upstairs pew'.

He charged his tenants in Port Erroll £2 and 10/- per year in rent for their cottages, and on the death of the head of the household let the resulting widows continue to live in their homes rent free. The family members were offered the cottage to rent before anyone else on the demise of the last parent.

Every year Earl Harry and his Countess, Eliza Amelia, gave a ball for the fishing people, and another ball for the farming people who lived in the estate's farms. It appears that this custom was retained by the following generations as there are records of a fishermen's ball in October, 1894. The music and dancing were interrupted when one of the coachmen heard a ship strike rocks beneath the castle. He immediately alerted the coastguard who called out the Port Erroll Rocket Brigade. The crew of the schooner-rigged steamship, *Chicago*, were all taken safely ashore by breeches buoy while the revellers from the ball looked on and cheered.

In 1891, Earl Harry died, and was followed by his son, Charles, who became 20th Earl of Erroll, Knight of the Thistle and Lord-in-waiting to King Edward VII. His Countess was Miss Mary Caroline L'Estrange.

Fourteen years previously when, in August 1875, Charles and his wife, then the newly married Lord and Lady Kilmarnock, came to Slains Castle after their wedding, there was great rejoicing throughout the Erroll estates. 'At every farm and cottage flags floated from chimney top and other prominent points.' The fishermen of the village of Ward were away at the herring fishing, but most of the Errolls' tenants were out to greet the young couple. The firing of signal guns, marking the progress of the open carriage drawn by four horses with outriders, could be heard for miles. The castle itself had bunting hung from turret to turret, a flag on the flagstaff, and, at both entrance gates were floral arches surmounted with floral coronets over which was set the falcon of the Errolls' legendary beginnings. At the one entrance 'Welcome' was displayed in evergreens and a table stood bearing the wedding gifts from the agricultural community, the fisherfolk, the pupils of Auchiries School and from the children who attended the Episcopalian Erroll Schools. The carriage, greeted by cheers and music from the band of the Cruden Volunteers, stopped at the table, and the minister of Cruden Parish Church, the Reverend R. Ross, presented Lady Kilmarnock with a silver-gilt epergne and two matching side pieces and Lord Kilmarnock with a jewelled gold ring on behalf of the farm tenants. From the fishing people Mr Ross presented them with an inscribed silver salver. The headmaster at Auchiries School gave the gift of his pupils – a 'Bible bound in dark brown morocco with gilt monogram and clasp of chaste design' and an ivory bound Church Service with a monogram and silver clasp. The teacher at the Erroll Schools, on behalf of the children, presented the couple with two books bound in dark brown morocco.

Some evenings later a ball, to which the estate tenantry were invited, was given by Lord and Lady Erroll to celebrate the marriage of this, their eldest son, Lord Kilmarnock. The castle was beautifully decorated in a similar fashion to that of the coming of age party of this young couple's eldest son, the next Lord Kilmarnock. 'The hall was most elaborately and tastefully decorated with evergreens, flowers, flags, banners, floral designs, family monograms and other devices connected with the family's history, past and present.' Wreaths of evergreens and flowers were twined round the balustrades of the staircase leading to the ballroom. 'On the landing of the first stair stood the figure of a lion-rampant, supporting the large silk ornamental flag of the castle. Garlands of evergreens, with stars in the centre, adorned each side of the staircase beyond this. On the second landing the word 'welcome' tastefully worked in moss, saluted the various guests as they arrived.' Refreshments were set out in side rooms. The new Lady Kilmarnock and her husband danced with most of the tenants. The hall, its walls on both sides 'draped with stripes of alternate pink and white cloth over which festoons of evergreens and flowers ran from end to end of the room', was said to be magnificent in 'the bright, dazzling glare of upwards of forty lights'.

Earl Charles was a professional soldier. Sir Iain Moncreiffe gave a resume of his military career.

As a Colonel he commanded the Royal Horse Guards (the Blues), as a Brigadier General he led an independent column in the Boer War, and in

1914 he commanded the Lowland Division as a Major-General. His long service in the State did not bring any money to meet the rising taxation and in the years between 1916 and 1922 he was forced sorrowfully to part with all the possessions held by his ancestors for so many centuries. He died in 1927.

Charles' Countess, Mary Caroline, was the one who 'cut the first sod' for the railway from Ellon to Cruden Bay. One cold September day in 1894, she put on a black satin dress, a green satin mantle trimmed with jet and a Reynold's hat with black feathers in her dressing room in Slains Castle. Down below in front of the castle, horses and carriages waited.

Eventually, a small party emerged and took their places in the vehicles. Lady Erroll joined her husband, Charles Gore, 20th Earl of Erroll, and her mother-in-law, the dowager countess, Eliza Amelia, and off they set on a journey of about 12 miles, which, in horse-drawn vehicles on untarred roads would have taken about three hours. Their destination was Ellon Railway Station where flags were flying.

As the horse-drawn procession travelled from the north, two special trains behind their steam engines chuffed from Aberdeen with between five and six hundred guests for the ceremony described in the newspapers as 'Cutting the First Sod'. It was a very short ceremony. Lady Erroll 'took hold of a little spade in a thoroughly workmanlike manner, and amid some cheers lifted some sods into a barrow'. She wheeled the barrow to the end of a wooden gangway, and toppled the sods from the barrow, and so started work on a railway line to Cruden Bay.

A marquee with flower decked tables inside waited in the grounds of Ellon Castle for the guests invited to the celebratory luncheon.

Earl Charles' and Lady Mary Caroline's son, Victor Hay, called after his godmother, Queen Victoria, was the young Lord Kilmarnock with whose coming of age celebration this chapter started. Sadly, he was not to continue the family line in Slains Castle which his father sold to Sir John Ellerman, the shipping magnate in 1916.

Victor Hay, 21st Earl of Erroll, KCMG was Charge d'Affairs in Berlin in 1919, and from 1921–27 held the position of British High

Commissioner, and ruled the Rhineland with the rank of Ambassador. He wrote a book entitled *Ferelith* which he based on Slains Castle, and in which he told a 'strange and sad' tale of a woman who had a ghost's child.

Victor was succeeded by his son, Josslyn Victor, 22nd Earl of Erroll, whose life in Kenya is written about in *White Mischief* by James Fox, and is a story of scandalous behaviour in the ironically named 'Happy Valley.'

His daughter was the late Lady Diana Denysa Hay, 23rd Countess of Erroll, who died in 1978. This Countess's first husband was Capt. Sir Iain Moncreiffe of that Ilk, Bt. PhD, who died in 1985.

Lady Diana once visited the place in Perthshire where her ancestors' original castle had stood eight centuries ago. As she approached the overgrown mound, 'corbies flew out rouping hoarsely, and there she found the grass growing on what had once been Erroll's hearthstone'. This event seemed to have brought true a prophecy of Thomas the Rhymer who lived near the end of the thirteenth century.

Quhile the Mistletoe bats on Erroll's Aik,
And that Aik stands fast.
The Hays sall flourish, and their guid gray Hawk
Sall nacht flinch befoir the Blast.
Bot quhen the root of the Aik decays
And the mistletoe dwines on its wither'd breast,
The grass sall grow on Erroll's Hearth-stane
And the Corbie roup in the Falcon's Nest.

Sir Iain Moncreiffe explains that this 'prophecy was literally fulfilled when, after the fall of the sacred oak [a mistletoe entwined oak tree that stood at Erroll in Perthshire], in the reign of Charles I, the lands of Erroll were sold out of the family'.

Sir James Frazer, quoting a Hay in *The Golden Bough*, explained that the badge of the Hays was the mistletoe, and that plant on the old oak in Perthshire held special meaning for the family.

It was believed that a sprig of the mistletoe cut by a Hay on All Hallows Eve, with a new dirk, and after surrounding the tree three times sunwise, and pronouncing a certain spell, was a sure charm against all glamour or witchery, and an infallible guard in the day of battle. A sprig so gathered was also put in infants' cradles to prevent the inmates being changed into elf-bairns by the fairies.

And so we come to the twenty-first century. At present, Lady Diana's son, Merlin, is 24th Earl of Erroll and the 28th of his family to hold the position of Lord High Constable of Scotland.

Lately, a newspaper reported that there is a scheme afoot to change the ruins of Slains Castle into holiday flats. This proposal has been given a mixed reception by local people. To some this would be sacrilege of a noble ruin; others, with a more practical turn of mind, argue that this would not, in fact, mean a boost to tourism in the village – people come to see the remains of the great house of Erroll. Who would come to look at holiday flats! Time will tell.

The Coming of the Railway

The 'Cutting the First Sod' ceremony in 1894 heralded perhaps the most dramatic era of change for Cruden Bay. After the Countess of Erroll played her part, the guests assembled for lunch in the flower bedecked marquee prepared for them in the grounds of Ellon Castle.

After lunch, there were several speeches all in an optimistic vein about the railway now to proceed from Ellon to Port Erroll, as Cruden Bay was then called. The railway was going to be a boon to the industries of the countryside which were fishing, farming and quarrying granite for which the area became well known. The railway company – The Great North of Scotland Railway (GNSR) – intended to make a golf course at Port Erroll and a splendid hotel for the numerous visitors expected to take advantage of the new means of reaching this part of the world. It was pointed out that now, as it would take only 12 hours to come from London to Port Erroll, it would be possible to breakfast in 'one of those important places and dine at the other'. The speaker explained that this fact contrasted greatly with what had been the case at the close of the last century. He had been reading 'that in 1796 the people of Aberdeen were rejoicing because the journey from there to Edinburgh had been reduced to 21 hours'. The audience laughed. He then went on to say – 'So far, I have only dwelt on the benefit which Cruden will derive from the improved communication with the outer world, but I cannot help thinking that there is another point of view from which it may be regarded, and that is the benefit which the world may gain from its closer connection with Cruden.' He caused more laughter when he illustrated this point by relating an amusing anecdote. 'I feel,' he said, 'somewhat like the Skye boatman who, when asked by an English tourist whether it was not the case that, during the winter, the island of Skye was two or three months cut off from all communication with London, said "Yes, but then you see it is just as bad for London."' He continued on the same theme by saying that he was of the opinion, 'That when Port Erroll is brought within 12 hours of London, the gain will not be entirely with the former, and that the jaded Londoner, worn out by his labours, either in the political, social or commercial worlds when he gets his first dip in the Bay of Cruden – [laughter] – that he will bless the Great North of Scotland Railway Company which has brought him within such easy reach of so ideal a spot.' The audience applauded.

Cruden Bay's Railway Station in times of prosperity

Mr Brand, the contractor, presented Lady Erroll with a miniature model of a railway wagon. It was in solid silver and had the arms of the Errolls inscribed on one side with the arms of the chairman, Mr William Ferguson of Kinmundy, on the other. On one end was a list of the railway company's directors and, on the other, the company's arms. It was to serve as a fruit or flower stand on the table at Slains Castle. Mr Ferguson said he was sure the wagon would be of more use than the wheelbarrow and silver spade, used by Lady Erroll during the ceremony, and presented to him by the contractor afterwards.

Five years after the cutting of the first sod it seemed that the dreams had come true and the optimism justified. There doesn't appear to have been any celebration to mark the railway's arrival at Cruden Bay Station nor its final completion at Boddam. The next ceremony of note was reported by *The Peterhead Sentinel and Buchan Journal* on 4 March, 1899. The preceeding Wednesday was the day when the Cruden Bay Hotel and adjoining golf course were officially opened.

The weather, for a March day, was delightfully fine and gave a pleasant foretaste of how charming a holiday will be at this new resort. From a bright blue sky, flecked with patches of fleecy clouds, the sun shone uninterruptedly, bathing the landscape in a flood of liquid light.

The hotel, with its finely dressed masonry, of delicate pink hue, stood out a handsome pile in the light of the brilliant day, and from the staves above large flags spread their ample folds to a pleasant breeze which bore on its wings a delicious and invigorating whiff of ozone. In the foreground lay the golf links, a fine stretch of sandy dunes abounding in hazards calculated to test the most experienced golfer in every department of the game, while here and there, like an oasis in the desert, could be detected a well-kept 'green', smooth as a billiard table, and affording scope for the utmost dexterity in 'putting'.

Beyond, was a magnificent sweep of the German Ocean in its most gentle mood, reflecting the tints of the passing clouds, and fringed with reefs and cliffs which constitute a most interesting bit of coast scenery. And closer investigation discovers other charms than those which a distant survey reveals. Between the two promontories that stand sentinel at the ends of the beautiful bay is a stretch of golden beach which opens up the most delightful possibilities in the way of bathing and boating, while a short distance either to north or south there are numerous creeks and caves in the rocks awaiting exploration by the enterprising tourist. Such are some of the attractions that await visitors to a district that is undoubtedly destined to become a popular resort.

In the vicinity of the hotel several rockeries were being prepared, and the reporter tells of the intention of planting 'a large quantity of trees and flowers'.

On the 9am train, Archie Simpson, the Aberdeen professional golfer, arrived to prepare for 22 gentlemen, members of Aberdeen Golf Club, who were coming to try the hazards of the new golf course. The expected golfers arrived in Cruden Bay on the 11am train. Later, a special train brought the directors and some chief officials of the Great North of Scotland Railway Company. Representatives of the local press had also been invited.

Everyone was taken on a tour of the Cruden Bay Hotel and all were suitably impressed by its grandeur. Again, *The Peterhead Sentinel and Buchan Journal* gives a full description:

The large hall and passages on the ground floor are thoroughly waxed and polished, and with the handsome settees and easy chairs and general surroundings open up a beautiful view to the visitor on entering.

The drawing room is a gorgeous apartment, covered with a magnificent carpet and upholstered with furniture of Chippendale mahoganay in Louis XV style. The coffee and breakfast rooms in the opposite wing are done up in a style similar to each other, and in the former 80 guests can be comfortably provided for. The chairs of both apartments are of a new design in fumed oak, with cane seat and back for lightness.

The billiard room is a well-lighted and comfortable apartment, while the writing room adjoining is simply but chastely furnished. The main stair-case is to be covered with velvet-pile carpeting, while the passages on the floors above are laid with cork carpets which makes a noiseless tread. These are large and commodious, the dark crimson dado gives them a cosy appearance, and they are provided with loungers and fancy coloured American cane chairs.

There are elegant and cheerful private parlours at the extremities of the building on the first floor; and the public bedrooms, both single and double, are finished with suites in walnut. The whole of the furniture has been made to match the general colours of the rooms, and they are substantial and extremely well made. The whole of the rooms are to be hung with lovely curtains, and when the tradesmen have left the building it will be one of the most handsomely appointed hotels in the country.

On a more prosaic level it was noted that all the bed and table linen, cutlery and other equipment was being stored away ready for the opening.

The late Mrs Bremner, wife of the Cruden Bay pharmacist, had been a guest at one of the balls held in the hotel. She recalled gliding down the red-carpeted staircase and admiring her silver-trimmed blue silk dress in the full length mirrors of the entrance hall. Her description of the hotel was 'magnificent'. I asked about the meal she'd had, but she couldn't remember. She said she'd been too excited to notice the food.

I spoke to Mrs Shearer who'd been a waitress. She told me that the food was excellent and that any special dish could be supplied by the French and Italian chefs. She described her uniform. It consisted of a navy blue *crepe de chine* dress, a small white apron fastened at the back with buttons (bows were not allowed), a little white cap, and stiff collar and cuffs. Every evening the waitresses had to 'stand like soldiers at their stations' for inspection by the head waiter. He checked their general appearance paying especial attention to nails and shoes. No make-up was permitted.

After the inspection, the head waiter beat the dinner gong, and into the blue and gold dining room came lords, ladies and gentlemen.

While dinner proceeded, the housemaids had to 'slop the rooms' – as Mrs Philips described the cleaning of wash bowls and ewers, and removal of the hot-water cans that the housemaids had brought to each room before dinner. Mrs Philips, then 14 years old, had to start work each day at 7am, and, apart from an afternoon break of two hours if work permitted, did not finish till 6pm. Those were her hours every day of the week. Her wage was seven shillings. She remembered, however, that some guests gave tips in the form of a weekly box of

Cruden Bay Hotel

chocolates, and occasionally after a lengthy stay a guest would give the housemaid as much as £10. I exclaimed, 'As much as that!', but Mrs Philips maintained it was so.

After dinner, guests would sometimes stroll over the links, and when cars became fairly common, parties would go to Aberdeen to the theatre or cinema. Some stayed in the hotel playing billiards in the 'well lighted and comfortable' billiard room, or sat in the 'simply and chastely furnished' writing room, or in the drawing room which was 'gorgeous with a magnificent carpet and upholstered with furniture of Chippendale mahogany in Louis XV style'. Sometimes the hotel residents organised a ball or concert to raise money for the poorer people in the village.

Very few of the villagers seemed to have ever been inside the hotel. Mrs Adams, who worked in the laundry to which the washing of all GNSR hotels was sent, told me that the nearest she ever got was the outside of the veranda where golf prizes were presented.

According to the 1908 *Guide Book*, 'The splendid golf course of 18 holes for gentlemen has been declared by prominent golfers to be one of the best in Scotland.' There is a short course of nine holes 'well patronised by ladies and beginners who were being taught by the resident professionals.

I understand the arrangement of the course has been considerably changed since those early days and perhaps the names of the holes as given in the 1908 *Guide Book* will be of interest to golfing enthusiasts. The first holes opened directly from the club-house. This was followed by Port Erroll, The Plain, Buckhole, The Downs, The Burn, The Cup, The Bunker and The Ravine. Then came the climb up Hawklaw by a flight of steps, known locally as 'Jacob's Ladder', at the top of which a seat was situated and a rest to appreciate the extensive view recommended. After this came, The High, the Valley, The Point, The Long, The Punchbowl, Hawklaw, The Gully, St Olaf and Home.

The names of guests who came year after year to the hotel and, in many cases, to play golf, sounded like a roll call of British business – Sir Jeremiah Colman of the famous mustard firm, Sir William Burrell of the Glasgow 'Burrell Collection' of artworks, the Gilbeys of port wine, the Wills of cigarettes, the McEwans of beer, the Crawfords of biscuits, tycoons of whisky companies, Swan Vesta matches, Bovril, Horlicks, Coats' thread and many more.

The village people seemed to remember Jeremiah Colman best of all. I spoke to Mr Cruickshank who had been one of his caddies. Usually about 100 boys waited eagerly to be employed by the caddymaster. On being chosen, the golfer paid one shilling for a caddy ticket and, at the end of the round, the caddy presented this ticket to the caddymaster, and received his payment of ninepence. There were no caddy cars in those days and instead of tees the caddy had to form a little cone of sand for the golfer to play off. When I first came to Cruden Bay, 40 years ago, there were still wooden boxes of sand set out on the golf course.

Sir Jeremiah Colman played every day of his holiday and on the last day told the caddy to bring his clubs to the hotel and ask for Lady Colman. Her ladyship would then appear and, with Sir Jeremiah hovering in the background, would thank the caddy, present him with half a sovereign if this was his first year, a whole sovereign on subsequent ones, would say, 'Hope to see you next year,' and then, much to the boy's embarrassment, would kiss him on the cheek.

One unique August Saturday afternoon in 1902 the village people were allowed to enjoy the hotel's environs. Children and adults assembled at the public hall, and, with two pipers leading them, marched to the front door of the hotel. They were received on behalf of the hotel guests by the Marquis and Marchioness of Headfort. 'His lordship read a telegram announcing that the King (Edward VII) had been crowned at 12.21pm amidst a scene of great splendour. The National Anthem having been sung, the sports commenced forthwith. Tea and other refreshments were supplied in abundance.'

We are not told if the village people were allowed to make use of the recreational facilities provided at the hotel for the amusement of the residents. I should think that unlikely. A GNSR advertisement in 1922 gives all the hotel's exterior advantages:

CRUDEN BAY HOTEL – Port Erroll
Finest air and finest Golf course in the Kingdom, Golf, Bowls, Tennis, Croquet, Boating, Fishing. Electric Tramway for Visitors between Railway Station and Hotel.

The guests could also reserve white bathing machines with black wheels which would be pulled down over 'stick roadies' to the beach by the coal-man's horse.

People responded well. Within months the 82 bedrooms provided were not enough and the Railway directors proposed the building of an extension to add 40 more bedrooms.

There were two electric tramcars which made their first appearance three months after the hotel opened. They transported guests from Cruden Bay's station, described as one of the most artistic stations on the whole railway. They must have been pleasant to look at, made of highly polished teak and furnished with gold velvet curtains and upholstery. They were each able to accommodate 16 passengers, whose luggage was carried on a raised platform at one end. This was where laundry baskets were carried as well. On Saturday, 25 June 1932, the trams ran as follows:

9.20–9.45am Passengers, 11.30–11.50am Luggage, 2.30–2.55pm Passengers, 2.55–3.15pm Luggage, 3.50–4.15pm Passengers, 8.10–8.35pm Passengers.

One of the trams has been reconstructed and can be seen in the Transport Museum at Alford, Aberdeenshire.

Inside, the hotel was electrically lit and equipped with a lift. It was a large, baronial style building described by one newspaperman as 'a palace on the sandhills'.

THE HARBOUR

In the first *Statistical Account* of 1792, Mr Cock, the minister of Cruden Parish Church, did his best to persuade the Earl of Erroll to take measures to provide the settlement, at that time called Ward of Cruden or The Ward, on the headland south of Slains Castle, with a proper harbour.

> If the small brook, formerly mentioned, could be carried into the sea at Ward, and a harbour made out that could receive small vessels, which might lie in safety at all seasons (of which there appears the highest degree of probability), a flourishing village would be the certain consequence. But if the bottom of the brook could be deepened, so as to receive such vessels as generally trade upon this coast, then, a very fine town would soon be built, and many a vessel saved, which, in time of danger or distress, durst not look at Peterhead, and would not be able to reach Aberdeen.

Mr Cock goes on to suggest that, if the Earl of Erroll set aside a monthly sum of money to carry out the necessary improvements:

> He would not only have the glory of improving and beautifying a large tract of country, but the satisfaction of being proprietor of one of the finest pieces of property in the North of Scotland.

The Earl of Erroll did not respond to Mr Cock's plea. When Mr Cock's successor, the Rev. Alexander Philip, wrote the second *Statistical Account* in 1840 he continued in the same vein as Mr Cock had done concerning the provision of a proper harbour. 'The harbour at The Ward can only be used in good weather,' he complained. 'But a safe and useful one could be made close by.'

In the Rev. Alexander Cock's time, Longhaven, Bullers o' Buchan, Ward and Whinnyfold had between them only eight boats, each crewed by six men and a boy when fully manned. Few of the boats, however, had enough men to make up a complete crew, and some boats were laid up. And though Dr Pratt (author of a history entitled *Buchan*) writes that, in 1798, the burn or stream had been diverted to enter the sea at Ward, the Rev. Alexander Philip noted in 1840 that the resulting harbour could only be used in good weather which was when boats bringing coal and lime called occasionally.

The making of a harbour had to wait till the latter half of the nineteenth century when, in 1875, Earl Harry, the 19th Earl of Erroll, undertook to provide one.

In 1872, Parliament consented to a Provisional Order made by the Board of Trade under the General Pier and Harbour Act of 1861. That same year, Queen Victoria confirmed the Order and, by so doing, gave William Harry Hay, Earl of Erroll, the authority to undertake the building of a harbour, so long as it conformed to the construction and administration rules as laid out in the Order.

The harbour, measuring about one and a half acres and consisting of two piers with a third middle pier, which divided it into an outer and inner basin, came into being between 1875 and 1880 and was soon being used by as many as 180 fishermen and 68 boats.

All ships coming into the harbour to load or unload paid fourpence per register ton. All ships windbound and having to shelter in the harbour, but not loading or unloading, were charged tuppence per register ton. Should the vessels import or export ale and beer, one shilling was charged on 50 gallons; the charge on bones of cattle was one shilling per ton; that on candles was tuppence per hundred-weight.

Provision was made in the Order for the laying down and

constructing of 'rails, tramways, sidings and turntables on and along the quays, piers and other works of the harbour and lands connected therewith'. From The Cruden Harbour Order, 1872, we can see that a great future was expected for this harbour and Earl Harry, on its construction, had the name of the village changed from Ward to Port Erroll.

In 1876, a lifeboat was stationed in Port Erroll. A lifeboat shed was erected, and a slipway constructed in front of it and down into the outer basin. In 1914, there was difficulty in finding enough men to crew the lifeboat so the station was closed down. It was brought into service again in 1915, but was permanently closed in 1921.

Before the Great War there were 16 big yawls manned by about 70 men and, some years before that, the village had 25–30 herring boats.

In 1916, Charles, 20th Earl of Erroll, had to sell his castle and lands. The buyer was Sir John Ellerman. In 1923, Sir John offered the harbour, which was in need of repair, to the local fishermen as a gift, together with £250 towards the repairs. They accepted and appointed three trustees to bear the responsibility of their gift.

Port Erroll's harbour in times of prosperity

Making a basket to hold baited fishing lines in Port Erroll in the distant past. In some parts this container is called a 'scull'.

However, in April 1928, a journalist from the *Weekly Journal* visited Port Erroll. He found a harbour in decline. There were only six motor boats working from the port, each with a crew of three or four men. Several boats lay idle on the wharf.

'Fishing will soon die out here,' an old man told the journalist, 'This was once such a brisk little village. At this time of the year all would be a bustle of preparation for the great line fishing.'

A wind of change had blown through the fishing industry. Sail had been replaced by steam; bigger boats able to go farther afield became the vessels of the day. 'If they would only give us a six-mile limit, we would make a success of it,' said one of the few young fishermen still remaining.

But the steam drifters and big trawlers were putting the small, inshore boats out of commission. Big boats could not use a small tidal harbour. Many Port Erroll fisherfolk moved to the big ports of Peterhead and Aberdeen. Many emigrated to America and the colonies.

Writing in 1929, Peter F. Anson tells how he, with his artist's pen and eye, came to Port Erroll. He described the harbour as having a look of abandonment and neglect. Grass grew on the unpainted piers, rotting boats lay about, their rusty chains and anchors beside them. In the statistical table he gives for 1928, we see that Port Erroll had two steam drifters, six motor boats, 11 under sail and 56 fishermen. Line and lobster fishing were still carried on.

At the end of the Second World War, the harbour was used by three seine-net fishing boats and a few small rowing boats owned by retired fishermen. (A seine net is, to put it very simply, a semi-circular net that is dragged along the sea bed.)

In 1960, about six small fishing boats were being charged 5/- a year and two to four large fishing boats £2 and 12/- a year.

The rights of the salmon fishers had been protected for all time when Sir John Ellerman handed over the harbour in 1923. In 1960, they were being charged £10 a year, as they had been since World War I. Ten years later, two small motor-boats fished with rippers and set creels, and from February to September two salmon cobbles set their bag-nets, sometimes as early as 4am, depending on the state of the tides.

The piers were badly eroded by 1971 and Col. Douglas Spratt headed a band of residents and Royal Engineers in an attempt to stop the rot. Only three small boats fished regularly from the harbour. 'Pier at Cruden Bay harbour is crumbling away,' was a heading in a local newspaper on 1 February, 1980.

In 1983, a Harbour Management Committee was formed. There had been a sudden rise in the number of boats using the harbour. The salmon cobbles were joined by yachts and other pleasure craft. Auction sales, dances, sponsored swims, Harbour Days were organised to raise funds to save the harbour. Backing in the form of large sums of money came from the Manpower Services Commission and the Scottish Tourist board while North East companies provided materials and equipment. However, in 1990, British Petroleum stepped in to deal with emergency repairs.

Grampian Enterprise with Banff and Buchan District Council, their eyes on tourism and a coastal walk to include Cruden Bay, gave the harbour environs a complete face-lift in 1993–94. The surfaces surrounding the harbour were concreted over, toilets were built, electricity power points were installed, a picnic and a look-out area was made. This last is known as the 'Loupin' Seat' for this place was so called in times past by the village people. It was here they had come to sit and watch dolphins leaping in the bay. Murmurs of caution were heard – the harbour itself was still in a very shaky condition.

The hard-working chairman of the Harbour Management Committee was under no illusion about the task undertaken by his committee. He compared the care of Cruden Bay Harbour to the eternal tending of the Forth Bridge.

Port Erroll, as Cruden Bay was called,
in the latter part of the nineteenth century

On the evening of 30 September, 1896, a special concert took place in the Port Erroll Public Hall. A grand piano had been obtained from Aberdeen, bills and tickets had been printed. For reserved seats – forms padded with flock-filled cushions – there were 100 tickets at 2/- each; 500 tickets for seating at the back of the hall, called 'Back form tickets', at 1/- each; and 70 Double tickets at 2/- were available for the concert and dance to follow.

W. J. Woodman Smith, commissioner for the Earl of Erroll, had assembled a Concert Party, for which he was to defray all expenses. He had planned a programme and had invited Charles Hay, 20th Earl of Erroll to preside, which his Lordship had consented to do. The platform was carpeted for the occasion. This event was to inaugurate the newly-built Port Erroll Public Hall.

First, Lord Erroll formally opened the Hall. The programme followed. The first part was devoted to religious pieces such as a quartette, which included Mr Woodman Smith, singing *Lord for Thy Tender Mercy's Sake* (Farrant); *The Holy City* (Stephen Adams) sung as a solo by Miss L. Christie of Aberdeen; and another solo – *Honour and Arms* (Handel) – again by Mr Woodman Smith. The second part, all secular music, included *A May Morning* (Denra); *Bedouin Love Song* (Pinsuti); *Annie Laurie* and ended appropriately with a quartette singing *Goodnight, Beloved* (Pinsuti).

What had been the Hall's forerunners? Where had the predecessors of Cruden Bay's inhabitants, the people of Ward of Cruden, and of Port Erroll, as the village was called from the 1870s to 1924, met for leisure and pleasure before the provision of the Public Hall?

According to some poems in a book entitled *Scots Poems*, published in Edinburgh in 1711, there was a meeting place for young blades 'at the end of the Earl of Erroll's Gate, between Slains Castle and Cruden Bay'. This was *Collegium Butterensi* – Buttery College – so called because the landlord of this tavern was called Peter Butter. From the poems we get a glimpse of life at Buttery College.

Initiation to the 'college' required the freshman to drink 'from a particular glass to every man he knew and then one more'. This test passed, he had to listen to an exhortation by Jacobus Hay Magistrum (or James Hay Master) on *artibus potabilibus* (the arts of drinking) *et* (and) *scientiis bibibilibus* (the knowledge of drinking).

The library was said to include 'Maximilian Malt-kist' on the principles of drinking, 'Mr Humphrey Hogshead' on the subject of devoted people – all titles given in Latin.

Did an actual meeting place in the parish inspire these poems, which were remarked on as showing 'wit, learning and humour' and of being 'altogether free from the coarseness which might have been expected in such a publication of that period'?

No doubt the habitues of the ten ale houses recorded in the district in 1840 had the same basic interest as the students of the Buttery College. But it wasn't all carousing. Harry Hay, Earl of Erroll from 1846–91, built a reading room in which a fire was lit all winter, reading matter and dominoes provided, but card games forbidden. This earl also started an Athletic Club; there was a gymnasium on Sandyhill Park north of the Congregational Church.

When, in 1894, the first meeting was held to consider the necessity for a public hall, it took place in the Mission hall built in the 1850s by public subscription for 'religious and educative purposes'. Subsequent meetings were held in the Infant School, the Lime Company's Stores and the Kilmarnock Arms Hotel. With such an assortment of venues for their meetings it's little wonder they reached the decision that a Public Hall was necessary.

It is noteworthy that to some of those meetings, when practical help was required, the all male committee brought their 'lady friends'. Fifty-five years were to pass before women, on their own suggestion, were elected to the Hall Committee.

Reaching the decision to build a Hall was the easiest part of the proceedings. Money had to be found, but of even more immediate concern was the need to obtain approval and, hopefully, a site from Charles Hay 20th Earl of Erroll. The Earl, approached through his commissioner, Woodman Smith, lived up to expectations, giving a site with a nominal feu duty and promising a donation of £20.

A Building Committee was formed. They visited the Public Halls at Newburgh and Mintlaw respectively, and so liked the Mintlaw Hall that they asked if they could borrow its plan and specifications for inspection – Mintlaw refused. The Building Committee then proceeded to have their own plans drawn up and sent to the Earl. His Lordship did not like them – the front gable was neither stylish enough nor ornate enough for his taste. The Earl had three sketches sent to the committee who chose Sketch No. 1, had a plan drawn up from it and sent the plan for the Earl's signature. It turned out that Sketch No. 1 was the work of Woodman Smith while Nos. 2 and 3 were according to the Earl's wishes.

The Committee, 'knowing that Lord Erroll will only sign No. 1 with dissatisfaction', decided to use Sketch No. 2. Then they changed their minds and bravely presented Lord Erroll with a modified version of No. 1. This time he signed.

Next came the raising of funds. On 25 August, 1894, a Bazaar was to be held on such a scale that there were appointed five committees – for Decorating, Amusements, Goods Distribution, Art Exhibition and Music. The admission charges were to be one shilling up to 2pm, sixpence to 6pm, threepence thereafter. The entrance fee for children was half price, exclusive of the minimum charge. The Coastguard was to be asked to lend flags and superintend their hanging. The many stalls on the day included ones selling flowers, china and toys. There were stalls for dairy produce, fish, refreshments, jumble and one called the Gentlemen's Stall. Listed on the advertisement were eight Patronesses and six Patrons who were members of the aristocracy and local gentry. Heading the list were the Earl and Countess of Erroll followed by the Dowager Countess of Erroll. Miss Buchan of Auchmacoy, the Rev. George Brown and Mrs Brown of Longhaven House and Col. and Mrs Russell of Aden all patronised the event.

The Bazaar raised £160. Cash on hand, promised but unpaid donations and surplus goods came to approximately £275. The Hall was expected to cost £400–500. Nevertheless, the Port Erroll Public Hall Committee went ahead and built their Hall. It was a courageous, laudable venture when, after all, there were only about 500 people in Port Erroll in the 1890s. In 1930, James Cruickshank, who had been convener from the start, informed the Inland Revenue that the total cost had been £730. Voluntary contributions had come to £319, and the balance had been borrowed from the Bank and private lenders on the security of the Hall.

An appeal was made to Andrew Carnegie to clear off the debts, but to no avail. Even Mr Coats, who had given libraries to many places, refused to gift books – surely a blow to the Literary Society.

Port Erroll Public Hall's Committee was on its own and on 28 September, 1896, it was decided to make up a Scale of Charges:

Local Concerts, Soirees & Similar Entertainments 10/-

Concerts other than local 15/-

Dramatic entertainments 15/-

Concert and dance £1

Ball £1

Marriage £1

Lecture 7/6

Political Meetings Day 15/- Night 16/6d

Dinners, Suppers etc. 10/-

Religious Service 5/-

Dancing classes 17 nights £2, or charge in proportion to number of nights

Ball to be charged £1 extra

The charges were to include fire, light and insurance, but if the range be used for cooking an extra two shillings and sixpence was to be charged. Local meetings for good of the Village and District were to be free, but the Secretary was to have a letter from a responsible party who would agree to make good any damage to the Hall.

Much use was made of the two ante-rooms. The Draughts Club used one regularly. In December 1897, the Hallkeeper recommended the purchase of a spitoon for each.

Before 1930 the Hall had no piano and one had to be hired from John Reid, a merchant in Port Erroll. For a full dance he charged 15 shillings and for a dance lasting two or three hours the piano's hire was 5 shillings. Mr Reid also gave Cinematograph entertainments and was charged 10 shillings for an afternoon's hire of the Hall.

Electricity, installed in 1929, was supplied by the local Brick and Tile Company and, in 1946, by an electricity supplier referred to as

'Grampian'. The existing petrol lamps were sold. Badminton and bowling were added to the activities.

The Hall Committee had to constantly raise funds so they held Strawberry Whist Drives, dramatic performances of such money pullers as 'Mains' Wooing' and Joe Corrie's 'Apron Strings', concerts, dances, and even a three-day Zoo brought by Mr Findlay of Cults all brought in revenue. The monkey and parrot are still remembered.

But there were hiccups. Boys broke windows; a picnic party jumped on forms till they were badly marked; someone forced the piano's lock; another drank a dance committee's aerated water; someone pulled the Freemasons' organ out of its case, and invaded the Oddfellows' wardrobe. There is truly nothing new under the sun. At one dance, washing powder was put on the floor instead of 'Slipperene'; even that august body, the Freemasons, damaged plaster with their secretive shutters; and, as for the military authorities, between 1939 and 1945 they had to pay more than £170 damages. They paid up and left, and afterwards Saturday night dances started in aid of a 'Welcome Home Fund' in preparation for the return of the village and district personnel from the Forces.

Extensive and frequent repairs and alterations were carried out throughout the life of the Hall, and reached a climax in the period 1978–80. Novel and hectic fund-raising prepared the way from March 1978. A 'Mr And Mrs' Competition, Top Team, discos, Treasure Hunt, Cheese and Wine evenings, a sponsored jog, and a Lend-a-Fiver-for-Two-Years scheme brought in considerable amounts of much-needed money. The renovations to the Hall were expected to cost £35,000–£36,000. Grants were available, and by 1980, the Committee had 75 per cent in actual cash of the 25 per cent of the amount they had to pay.

The project had escalated tremendously from the time it was first mooted. Instead of having to please an Earl of Erroll, as had been the case a century ago, Grampian Regional Council had to be satisfied with the conduct and results. A booklet of August 22, 1979, setting out the proposals of design and work, concludes: 'From the initial work undertaken in the design of the scheme as presented, it would appear that what was originally envisaged as a small alteration has owing to the conditions being set forth by Grampian Regional Council, become a major works.'

The activities and charges in 1996 read somewhat differently from those of 1896.

Port Erroll Public Hall Hire Charges

Normal club activities are charged £2 per hour with £3.50 extra per session for Heating.

Local organisations raising club funds or donations to charity pay £19 including heating.

Local people holding a disco pay £38 including heating – £50 if the Hall is not left clean and tidy.

£50 is the fee for selling goods commercially with heating extra at £3.50 per session.

Local or non-local groups benefiting financially from their activities – £8 per hour, with heating at £3.50 per session added on.

Ante-rooms are still used for small meetings lasting not more than 2 hours, and for those there is a flat charge of £2 plus 65p for heating.

Those various categories embrace – concerts, coffee mornings, performances by the junior and senior drama groups, and various other functions.

As the Hall's centenary was celebrated, the main activities for which it was used were – A Mother and Toddler Group, a Playgroup, School Physical Education Lessons, Dancing Classes, SWRI meetings, Badminton, Bowling and the Over-50s Club.

It could be said that the Port Erroll Public Hall caters for the inhabitants of Cruden Bay and nearby district from life's morning to its twilight.

Port Erroll Public Hall was not the only building site granted by the Errolls and, usually, on giving or renting land they also gave a subscription to help with payment for the construction.

In 1834–35, William George Hay, 18th Earl of Erroll, and his wife, the Countess Elizabeth, founded the Erroll Schools so called for the building was divided in two – one section being the Boys' School and the other the Girls' School.

They also helped financially towards the re-building of St James the Less in 1843. This Episcopalian church stands on a hill by the main road southwards from Cruden Bay to Aberdeen. Though this actual building only goes back to the nineteenth century, Episcopalianism had had a turbulent fight for existence since the early eighteenth century.

When we first read of churches in the parish of Cruden it is of pre-Reformation times when Roman Catholicism ruled supreme. Then came the throwing off of the Papal supremacy and Episcopalianism took its place, accepted with great reluctance it would seem by Earl Francis at Slains Castle. This Earl was excommunicated because he refused to conform to Protestantism. Because of his Roman Catholic sympathies he was confined to his castle and a certain radius round it for some years. However, in 1617, King James VI repealed those restrictions since the Earl had recanted to the satisfaction of the Church authorities. However, in 1620 we read that he was ordered to appear before the Lords of the Privy Council because he had sent his son to France accompanied by a known Roman Catholic. Again, Earl Francis seems to have been forgiven his rebellious behaviour against the established Episcopalian church, and it was believed that when he died in 1631, the last traces of Roman Catholicism in the area were extinguished. The Erroll family then supported Episcopalianism through the generations.

Their staunchness to this faith appears especially in Countess Mary, 14th of the line. Trying times were facing Episcopalians. Their religion was being forced out by Presbyterianism which did not hold with bishops and hierarchical government of the church. The Presbytery was to be all powerful. When Mr Dunbar, the last Episcopalian minister in the Parish Church of Cruden was dismissed, he left the area for good, leaving behind a resolutely loyal congregation. Countess Mary had a granary on the farm of Ardendraught converted into a chapel for Dunbar's now churchless following. Presbyterians named this place of worship 'Countess Mary's Girnal' and here the Episcopalians met till after the 1745 Jacobite Rebellion when Hanoverian dragoons set fire to the chapel and burned it, including all its contents.

The Jacobite Cause was espoused by the majority of Episcopalians and this gave the Hanoverians a good excuse to have done with them. Great efforts were made to find Mr Dunbar blatantly supporting Jacobitism and so have good reason to remove him. Members of his affectionate congregation were compelled to answer questions about his conduct in church under threat of being fined one hundred merks if they dared refuse. It is obvious from their answers the testifying against their popular minister was done with great reluctance.

One parishioner, Thomas Smith of Greenhill, maintained that he had never heard Mr Dunbar pray for King George by name, but nor had he ever heard him pray for the Pretender as King James VIII. He had heard him pray that the King might again be on his ancestral throne. He had heard him pray for the King, whether it was the man at sea or on land, during the time of the 1715 rebellion, but could not remember if he had done so after the Pretender had arrived on British soil. He could not recall Mr Dunbar saying that Usurpers had taken over the throne. Smith did admit that the minister used a liturgy in the church and kept it in the manse.

In the warrant issued in 1716, Mr Dunbar was described as an 'intruder' and the military authorities were commanded to march to the church and remove him.

Church and school were closely linked in those days, and after Mr Dunbar's deposition in 1716, and departure from the parish in 1718, Mr Keith, the schoolmaster, took over his job as well as continuing in his own. For at least another four years he was minister and schoolmaster. Then he resigned from the school and devoted himself to his Episcopalian flock.

When a Presbyterian minister had been appointed to replace Mr Dunbar, the Presbytery had appealed to Mr Keith (then schoolmaster as well as minister to Episcopalian dissenters), to discipline some of his schoolboys whom the new minister complained of committing 'gross abuses' during his services. One wonders how much of the requested disciplining Mr Keith actually administered.

Episcopalian worship ran into more difficulties in Mr Keith's time during which the '45 rebellion took place. A law was passed forbidding Episcopalians from having gatherings of more than four people in addition to the immediate family. In response, Mr Keith moved into a farmhouse called 'Sandend'. On Sundays the congregation assembled on the grass at the front of the house and four people joined Mr Keith and his family in the parlour. Then the window was taken out. Thus, Mr Keith was able to speak to those inside and also be heard by the assembly outside. Mr Keith died in 1763.

The schoolmaster at the time of the '45, Charles Gordon, was also suspected of Jacobitism. He was called before the Presbytery and accused of permitting the scholars to wear white cockades, of drinking 'my Prince's health', and of saying – Gordon maintained only in jest – 'Oh if we had but 300 Highlanders' when Hanoverian troops arrived to hunt down some Frenchmen who had been landed at the Sands of Ardendraught. It was mainly because the pro-Jacobite Mary, Countess of Erroll, intervened that Charles Gordon was allowed to retain his job.

The Rev. Adam Mackay, telling of those events, states that the parish school stood 'about 50 yards north of the Bishop's Bridge'. He gives this information when talking of a pupil called Robert Kilgour. This pupil went to King's College, Aberdeen, where he graduated with an MA. Eventually, he became an Episcopalian Bishop. An earlier pupil, Patrick Gordon, attended the school 'at the kirk of Crochdan'. After a very chequered military career, during which he fought for any country that would employ him, he rose to the rank of general in the army of Czar Peter the Great of Russia. Patrick Gordon had a close relationship with the Czar. Indeed, it was written that when Gordon died in 1690, 'the eyes of him, who left Scotland a poor unfriended wanderer, were closed by the hands of an Emperor.' He was buried with the greatest pomp and ceremony, the Czar himself being present at the funeral. It would seem that though political peace often did not reign in Cruden's parish school, it turned out pupils who made their mark in later life.

This school being in the vicinity of the Bishop's Bridge meant it was situated about the centre of the parish and at quite a distance from the village. The Bishop's Bridge had been erected by Bishop Drummond, a relative of Lady Anne Drummond, Countess of Erroll, helped by the Earl of Erroll. The Bishop, a friend of the Jacobite minister, Mr Dunbar, had been deprived of his see when Presbyterianism replaced Episcopalianism. Lady Anne had invited him to make his home in Slains Castle. He had become perturbed about the parishioners having to ford the Water of Cruden when in spate to reach the church, and so determined to build a bridge in 1690. Consequently, the bridge was named after him. Bishop Drummond's arms and those of the Earl of Erroll are inserted in one side of the bridge. When Bishop Drummond died, he left his book collection to the Earl and it became part of the castle's library.

Probably because both church and school were at a considerable distance away, the village people wanted a church and later a school in the village. Earl Harry promised a free site for a Congregational Church and manse in 1882, and in 1887 the villagers petitioned him for an Infant School. When the Rev. Alexander Philip wrote the *Statistical Account* in 1840 there were as many as five schools – the one near the Church and 'four unendowed schools in convenient situations'.

It was not till 1903 that the recently closed school was opened. In September, 1955, it was a junior secondary with four full-time teachers, one visiting teacher and 87 pupils. The Erroll Episcopal School had at that time 19 pupils. At Port Erroll School domestic and technical courses had been added to the curriculum. The Rev. R. R. Robertson, author of the third *Statistical Account* published in 1960, commented that the school broadcasts, the use of the gramophone, cinema film strips, slides and the epidiascope were 'perhaps the greatest changes in the classroom'. He also drew attention to the fact that there had been progress in school conditions. School sanitation, health service, heating had all improved and, when he wrote, electricity was being installed. For the head teacher there was now a telephone.

The 1903 building, which celebrated 100 years as a school in 2003, closed at the end of the summer term. Since 1978 only infant classes were taught there. In 2003, a 'state of the art' school, costing £3 million, was opened to accommodate all ages of primary children.

The Congregational Church and manse remain. The church stands nearly at the end of Main Street and the manse (now a private dwelling) is situated on the main road through the village to Peterhead to the north, and Aberdeen to the south.

The present Parish Church of Cruden was built in 1776. According to the first *Statistical Account,* written by Rev. Cock, it was built 'out of one stone, upon which hallow fires formerly used to be burnt, and which also served as a landmark to fishers, when at sea, being upon the top of a gravelly eminence.' At the time of Rev. Cock's writing, the Earl of Erroll was patron, and the minister was paid £35, 11 shillings, one penny and four twelfths pence in money, 48 bolls of meal and 16 bolls of bere, and had a six acre glebe, 'a manse and offices'. The Earl of Erroll had instigated an extension of the church and the replacement of the manse which Mr Cock describes as 'very old and ruinous'.

We read no more of the Earl's renovation plans at that time, but in 1834, the church was radically altered and among other additions was given its round towers, 'which,' Adam Mackay remarks, 'give it its unique appearance'. It is thought that when Slains Castle was practically rebuilt in 1836, its similar towers were to the design of the same person responsible for those of the church. In 1843, St James the Less Episcopalian Church was also altered to the shape we see today.

Neither St James the Less nor the Parish Church have sailed unruffled through the years. St James the Less saw a struggle between English and Scottish Episcopalianism and the Parish Church endured the upheaval of the Disruption when a breakaway occurred and a Free Church was built in the village of Hatton. Its congregation comprised those who believed that the Church Presbytery should be free to accept or reject ministers and not have them chosen by a patron. A great number of ministers and their congregations left the established church over the heads of this bone of contention. Mr Philip of Cruden was one of the dissenters in 1843. A large number of his congregation followed him.

The first Sunday after the split, the Free Church faction held its service in a barn at the farm of Stones. By the next Sunday a wooden church had been erected for them beside the Mill of Hatton.

Much bad feeling was aroused by the Disruption, enough, in fact, for people of both churches to push and jostle their opponents and not allow free passage to whichever church was their destination. Nevertheless, Mr Shepherd of the farm of Aldie, a great-great grandfather of the present-day newspaper tycoon, Rupert Murdoch, remained loyal to the established church and behaved well. He granted a feu of about two acres for an annual nominal rent of £1 to the Free Church people, and there they built their stone church which, though not architecturally attractive, could hold 800 people. Rupert Murdoch's grandfather, the Rev. Patrick Murdoch, before emigrating to Australia, ministered in this United Free Church. He is given the credit of rebuilding the church in a much more attractive style. It was opened in 1885.

STORY OF THE VILLAGE

When Mr Cock, the Parish Church minister, wrote the first *Statistical Account* in 1792, Ward of Cruden was so insignificant he mentioned it along with three other settlements. 'There are four villages or sea towns, altogether occupied by sea-faring people, and consequently situated along the coast, viz. Long-haven, Bu'ler's Buchan, Ward and Whinnyfold. None of them are very populous, having been much neglected of late.' The situation does not appear to have altered greatly when, in 1840, the Rev. Alexander Philip wrote the second *Statistical Account*. All he had to say about the villages was – 'There are no villages in the parish except those of Bullers-Buchan, Ward and Whinnyfold, which all belong to the Earl of Errol.'

Both Mr Cock and Mr Philip have no qualms in claiming that Cruden got its name from a battle on the links of Cruden Bay in 1005 when Malcolm II of Scotland fought and defeated Canute, a prince of

Denmark, and his invading Danes. In 1858, Dr Pratt is of the same opinion as to the origins of the name 'Cruden', stating that it came from *Croich Dane*, 'the slaughter of the Danes'. However, since those perhaps more credulous days, grave doubts have been cast on past accounts of how the parish, and later the village, came by their name.

Those past historians and many others before them, have based their accounts on the reportage of Boethius, who lived 1465–1536 and described a battle on the links most vividly and in considerable gory detail. But Boethius stands accused of embellishing facts, presumably to make a lively story. It is now generally believed that there was perhaps some sort of skirmish on Cruden Bay's links, but not a battle of great note between Nordic invaders and the Scots. However, it must be pointed out that Dr Pratt wrote that there were still grave mounds all over what was known locally as the 'Battle Fauld', and that a farmer in his time levelled the mounds with his plough – an action deplored by Dr Pratt. It is also worthy of note that Erasmus, a friend and contemporary of Boethius, described the latter as one who 'knew not what it was to make a lie'; that the locals called a stream on what became the Golf Course 'The Bleedy Burn'; and that the Danish Royal House paid the Erroll family an annual sum to tend the grave of a prince buried here. A large limestone slab in the present churchyard was said by Dr Cock to have lain on a Danish prince's grave.

Mr Cock also mentions that there was at one time a Danish castle on the links, and both he and Dr Pratt believed that when King Malcolm made peace with the Danes, he promised among other things to build a church on the scene of battle, and dedicate it to the patron saint of Denmark, St Olaf. This dedication must, however, have taken place much later than the erection of a church, for Olaf, who became Denmark's saint, did not die till the Battle of Sticklestaad in 1030.

Boethius claims that Malcolm's church was 'ouircassen be violent blast of sandis', and a replacement was built at another site. Dr Pratt reported that the remains of a church stood in the vicinity of what nowadays is Cruden Bay Pharmacy. It has been written at later dates that these ruins were what was left of the original St Olaf's church, and that there never was another nearer the shore which could have been blown over by sand. The replacement church is believed to be where the present parish church is now situated. Perhaps the Time Team should be invited to solve the confused tale of Cruden's early churches!

Mr Cock talked of a past village. 'None of the houses of the village now remain. But some of the hearth stones, with ashes upon them, were dug up some time ago in casting a ditch for an enclosure.' This village he positioned near where Malcolm's chapel had been built; and he said it was 'called *Croju-Dane* or *Cruden*, which signifies, "kill the Dane".' This is the second reference to a village that I have found. The first mention of one is made in a poll taken in 1695 when 'Seamen in Wairdhill' were said to have numbered 21. In 1875 the population is given as 'over 200'.

The Rev. Alexander Philip, as has been said, simply gave the names of three villages existing in 1840. Dr Pratt tells us little more. He said Cruden used to be called Invercruden which he said means 'Cruden near the mouth of a stream'.

As to the mystery of the name: others are of opinion that it was called Cruden, or Cruthen, because it formed part of the ancient Cruthenica or Pictish kingdom, so called from Cruthen, the first king of the Picts.

Dr Pratt, however, quotes a writer called Bellenden:

King Malcolme, havand his realm in sicker peace, thocht nothing sa gude as to keep the promes maid to Danis; and thairfore, he biggit ane kirk at Buchquhane, dedicat in honour of Olavus, patron of Norrway and Denmark, to be ane memoriall that sindry noblis of danis wer sumtime buryit in the said kirk. In memory heirof, the landis, that ar gevin to this kirk, ar callit yet, Croivdan , qyhilk signifyes als mekil as the slauchter of Danis.

As has already been mentioned, Dr Pratt's sources – Bellenden and Abercrombie – having got their information from Boethius, who is suspected of embellishing the truth, have had doubt as to their authenticity cast upon them by later historians.

When in 1912 the Rev. Adam Mackay, incumbent of Cruden Parish Church, wrote *Cruden and its Ministers*, he reported that 'There are those still alive who can remember when Port Erroll consisted of a mere line of houses scarcely extending 50 yards along the shore near the mouth of the burn.'

However, by 1912 great changes had come about in Port Erroll. It now had 'three general merchants, a baker, a butcher, a fish merchant, a shoemaker, a chemist, two tailors, a carpenter, a blacksmith and a builder'. There was a 'post office, public hall, bank, church, school and hotel', namely the Kilmarnock Arms. Adam Mackay said the Cruden Bay Hotel could not be said to be in the actual village. A brickworks had replaced two earlier ones in 1902. To clothe these bare facts with flesh and blood, we may look at the guide books published in 1907 and 1908, each costing threepence.

In these books, Cruden Bay was described as 'The Brighton of Aberdeenshire', and the Cruden Bay Hotel, largely the cause of this description, was impressively pictured. Other factors included the coming of the railway and the golf course. There is also a picture of the Kilmarnock Arms Hotel and its facilities are advertised as – shooting, fishing, golf, motor garage with pit, petrol, hiring, stabling, billiards, postal and telegraph office in the hotel.

The Kilmarnock Arms Hotel was a popular venue for visitors long before the village became a tourist resort. In 1893, it had a guest who was to become famous – Bram Stoker, best known as the writer of the classic tale, *Dracula*. His biographer, H. Ludlam, tells us that Stoker 'walked into the village that squatted beside the Water of Cruden, past the few rows of fishermen's cottages with two or three great red-tiled drying sheds nestled in the sand dunes behind them.' A writer of about the time Bram Stoker first came says about the cottages: 'very decent and comfortable looking and all seemed to be well furnished with a more than usual assortment of mugs and jugs and plates and other crockery'. The population was then about 200.

Bram Stoker made for the Kilmarnock Arms – 'the one small hotel down on the western bank of the Water of Cruden with a fringe of willows protecting its sunken garden full of fruits and flowers.' H. Ludlam tells us that Stoker spent hours with the coastguard in his look-out. This we may well believe, for the story he started that summer, and finished on his return the following year, had as its hero Sailor Willy, a young coastguard on watch in the look-out on the north cliff above Port Erroll. Willy was engaged to be married to Maggie, daughter of a local fisherman.

For the reader of their tragic story, *The Watter's Mou,* the place below the ruins of the old barley mill, where the Back Burn flows into the sea, will forever be haunted by Maggie and Willy. After the story's completion, its author wrote in the visitors' book of the Kilmarnock Arms: 'Second visit – delighted with everything and everybody and hope to come again.'

His hopes were realised. In August 1895, he was to be seen striding across the two-mile stretch of flat, tawny sands or sitting on the rocks at the far end of the beach, gazing at the treacherous Skares of Cruden and at the hamlet of Whinnyfold perched on the cliff tops above these dangerous rocks.

Seemingly, he was not a comfortable companion throughout this visit, for he was obsessed with a new idea, and was not pleased if his brooding was interrupted. Before the holiday was over, he had written the first chapters of *Dracula*. It is widely believed that the story was inspired by Slains Castle. There is in the castle an octagonal inside walk-way, and in Castle Dracula there is an octagonal room. It would seem feasible that Stoker borrowed the castle's eight-sided area for his book.

Dracula was published in May 1897. Three months later, Bram Stoker and his family were back in Cruden Bay, and this time the inspiration for a new story came directly from his holiday venue. In this tale, Cruden Bay appeared as 'Crooken Sands' and the village as 'Mains of Cruden' or the 'Port of Crooken'. The Skares were renamed the 'Spurs'. The holidaying family of the story resided in the 'Red House', which I take to be our present-day Red House Hotel.

In another story set in Cruden Bay, Stoker made no attempt to disguise it or hide his feeling for it. His hero speaks the deep-felt thoughts of his creator when he says, 'When I first saw the place I fell in love with it.'

Throughout 1900 he worked at *The Mystery of the Sea*. The hero, Archie Hunter, like Bram Stoker, stayed in the Kilmarnock Arms. It was on the bridge beside the hotel that Archie first experienced second sight and 'saw' a coffin being carried across the bridge. Here, too, he met the mysterious gipsy, Gormala, who'd shared his vision.

To the reader of *The Mystery of the Sea*, the beach and dunes between the cruel Skares and St Olaf's Well on the golf course will always be the place where a procession of the drowned wound its slow way from the surging sea to enter the bubbling waters of the well.

A literary guide states: 'There is a fascination about places associated with writers.' That Bram Stoker visited Cruden Bay from 1803–1910 adds a dimension of interest to the locality for resident and visitor alike.

From an old board showing charges, which the proprietors of the Kilmarnock Arms showed me in the 1970s, I discovered that the hero of *The Mystery of the Sea* would have paid threepence a day for stabling his bicycle while he was lodged in the hotel. Had he possessed a horse, the charges would have been: sixpence for stabling for less than four hours, 3/- for overnight with two feeds of oats and hay, and 5/- for 24 hours with four feeds.

A question frequently asked is, how did the Kilmarnock Arms in Cruden Bay, a far distance from the town of Kilmarnock, get its name? As with most places in Cruden Bay there is a link through the Errolls.

When Mary Hay, 14th Countess of Erroll, died in 1758, she was succeeded as 15th Earl of Erroll by her great-nephew, James, Lord Boyd, who took the family name of Hay. The coat-of-arms displayed outside the Kilmarnock Arms Hotel is that of James' father, William Boyd, Earl of Kilmarnock. This 4th Earl of Kilmarnock, having switched allegiance from the Hanoverian to the Jacobite side, was taken prisoner at Culloden. His son, James Hay, 15th Earl of Erroll, fought for King George and when his father was led away, a hatless prisoner, James stepped from the victorious ranks and placed his own hat on his father's head.

Lord Kilmarnock was beheaded on Tower Hill. At his execution it is alleged that he wore an ornament known as the Kilmarnock Jewel in his bonnet. The jewel consisted of a large diamond in the centre surrounded by a cluster of small precious stones. According to legend, as Lord Kilmarnock's head fell, the diamond was transformed into the blood red ruby which is in the Erroll family's possession. It was thoughts of the unfortunate Earl that made James Boswell feel uneasy during his uncomfortable night in Slains Castle. He feared the poor gentleman might put in an appearance.

In the next century, the 1800s, William George Hay, 18th Earl of Erroll, was granted the British Peerage of Lord Kilmarnock. In 1897, the eldest son of the then Earl of Erroll, the 20th of the line, had the title Lord Kilmarnock. Following this gentleman, who became 21st Earl, the title passed to his second son, Gilbert (his elder son, Josslyn Victor, being titled Lord Hay). Thereafter, the Kilmarnock title passed down through the descendants of Gilbert.

The guide books bring to life the doings of the ordinary people of the village. The increased tourism brought custom and employment. Private houses were let to visitors. Fishermen – especially those no longer going to the herring or line fishing – became boatmen who took tourists fishing or pleasure boating. 'Parties taken out for sailing or fishing by the hour or day,' offered David Tait and Charles Masson who used boats called *Emmanuel, Togo* and *Nile.* Rods and tackle could be hired and bait was supplied.

George Milne and Sons, who were carpenters, joiners, house painters, decorators, ironmongers and general house furnishers, besides selling 'perambulators, mailcarts, beds, mattresses and household furniture of every description', would hire out those items. They also had bathing coaches for hire, and urged at the foot of their advertisement – 'Also other Novelties – Dinna forget to send away Souvenirs to your friends, besides securing a Memento for yourself'. R. T. Smith, tailor and outfitter, said that he made 'Costumes and suits for tourists, Golfers and all Holiday Makers, from 35/- to 5 guineas'. His garments were made of Harris tweeds, serges and flannels, and he ended his advertisement with 'Testimonials – Lady – "My costume is beautiful; everybody admires it",' and 'Professional Golfer – "My Suit is splendid, and fine for golfing"'. John Reid, Grocer, Draper and Ironmonger on Main Street also offered 'Dressmaking and Millinery'.

Adam Mackay says the population in 1912 was 616, and business for the hoteliers and merchants appeared to be booming. However, it was a different story for the village's main occupation, the fishing industry, which, as described in the Harbour chapter of this book, was in irrevocable decline.

Other changes too were afoot. Perhaps an early hint of a new era breaking was seen in 1916 when an advertisement containing the following and many more items appeared in a newspaper:

An interesting collection of historical relics from Slains Castle has been consigned to Mr Milne of the Bon Accord Auction rooms, Aberdeen, for sale by private bargain

Pocket handkerchief of Frederick Duke of York who died in 1827; Pair of gloves worn by William IV on opening his first Parliament; Stone thrown at William IV at Ascot Heath races by a mad sailor; Two feet of last horse (Bushy) ridden by King Wm. 4th.

Slains Castle, home of the Hays of Erroll was up for sale. Twentieth-century taxes and death duties forced Charles Hay, 20th Earl of Erroll, to sell to Sir John Ellerman the ship-owner. Sir John is said to have never even visited the Castle while he owned it. He rented it in the summer months to such people as the Earl of Oxford and Asquith and to Dame Clara Butt, the famous singer, and her husband. Many years later people could remember hearing from as far way as the village Dame Clara singing at the castle on summer evenings. In 1923, Sir John Ellerman sold it to Mr Percy P. Harvey of London who gifted the village the recreation park, the site of their Public Hall and Mission Hall. From 1923–25 the castle was occupied by a caretaker and his family, and in 1925 it was dismantled and its roof removed.

Previous to each change of ownership, large farms were sold, largely to their occupying tenants. The salmon fishing was bought by a Peterhead firm. A sale catalogue of 1922 gives a picture of the castle as it was at the time Ellerman put it on sale, and the extent of the estate he had acquired from the Errolls.

LOT 1.

PARTICULARS OF THE CRUDEN ESTATE

With Slains Castle, Low Ground shooting, Farms, Trout Fishing, Cruden Bay Golf Links, the Village of Port Erroll, and net Salmon Fishings in the Sea. Extending to an area of about 4,200 acres.

SITUATION

The Cruden Estate lies into and includes Cruden Bay on the Aberdeenshire Coast, about 20 miles North of Aberdeen and 5 miles South of Peterhead. Cruden Bay Station on the Ellon to Boddam System of the Great North of Scotland Railway is on the Estate.

AREA

The estate extends to an area of about 4200 acres.

SLAINS CASTLE

(the principal Residence on the Estate) is situated within its own Grounds, and is substantially constructed of Aberdeenshire Granite. It dates from 1654, but was rebuilt according to more modern principles in 1837. The Castle occupies a unique position on a precipice overhanging the Sea, and commands magnificent Cliff and Sea Views towards the South. On the Landward side, the Castle is fronted with wide terraced lawns and flower beds. Approached by two Carriage Drives, the Castle contains the following accommodation: 7 Reception Rooms, 14 principal Bed and Dressing Rooms, 2 Bathrooms, 4 w.c.s, and ample Domestic Offices, disposed as follows:

On the Principal Floor – Entrance Hall (heated with stove) leading to Central Octagonal Interior Hall (heated with stove and lighted from roof) from which open the following lofty Reception rooms:- Drawing Room (38ft. 6 ins. by 20 ft. inclusive of Bay) with South-east aspect and finely decorated ceiling. Dining Room (36 ft. by 24 ft.), a handsome Room facing North-east, with coved ceiling, Library and Billiard Room (30 ft. by 19 ft exclusive of Bay), facing East and South-east, richly panelled with Oak and fitted with Book Shelves. Ante Room between Drawing Room and Library, Suite of Bedroom, Dressing Room and Bathroom with Lavatory Basin and w.c., 9 Bed and Dressing Rooms, 3 w.c.'s, Bathroom, Housemaid's Pantry and Butler's Pantry.

Below the Principal Floor, but on the ground level, reached by Principal and Secondary Staircase are – Smoking Room facing South-east with Bay window overlooking the Sea, Boudoir with South and East aspect with door leading to Cliffs, Fernery, 3 Bedrooms, w.c., Housekeeper's Room, Sewing

Room with Lady's Maid's Bedroom off, Servants' Hall, Silver Room, 8 Servant's Bedrooms, Kitchen, Scullery, Cook's Larder, Pantry, Boot Hall, Boiler House, Coal Cellar, Coal House, Wine Cellar, Beer Cellar, Drying Room, Washing House, Laundry.

Lighting – The Castle is lighted by Lamps.

Central Heating – A Hot Water Heating System is installed.

Water Supply – There is a good Supply of Water by gravitation to Cisterns in the roof of the Castle.

Drainage – The sewage is piped into the sea, and the system has always proved thoroughly satisfactory.

Stabling, &c. – Outside and adjoining the Castle are – Harness Room with Laundry and 2 Bedrooms over, Stables comprising 10 Stalls and 2 Loose Boxes, Two Garages for 3 Cars with Inspection Pit, Coachman's House with 2 Rooms and Kitchen, Old Washing House with ample Loft accommodation. Office or Rent Collection Room.

The Gardens and Grounds – To the South and West of the Castle are wide terraces with trimmed Lawns, suitable for tennis and Croquet, and Flower Beds, while there is a terrace walk above the cliffs, and towards the South is a lookout Bastion with old guns.

The Castle and the terraces are enclosed by walls with handsome balustrades, columns, and iron gates.

A short distance from the Castle are the pretty walled-in Flower and Kitchen Gardens, divided both by trimmed thorn hedges and a trouting stream which is crossed by foot-bridges. In the Gardens are two Vineries, a Glass house, Potting Shed, Barrow Shed, Store Shed, and Gardener's Bothy. Beyond the Kitchen Garden is a grove of Chestnut, Sycamore, and Ash Trees, through which a path leads to the Lower Garden, where there are two Lawns, Fruit Trees, and Shrubs. Shady Walks lead into the Crow Wood. Close to the Gardens is a Gardener's House, containing three rooms and kitchen, and another Cottage suitable for a gamekeeper.

AGRICULTURAL

Besides the Home Farm, there are twenty-eight Farms and several smaller Holdings. The Farms are equipped with substantial buildings in good order. The land throughout varies from a light loam to a stiff red clay.

SPORTING

Shooting – The Low ground Shooting over the Estate extends to about 4200 acres. The Estate has been very lightly shot over during the last few years, and no proper records of Game Bags have been kept, but in a good season it is estimated that roughly 80 to 90 brace of Partridges, 80 brace of Snipe, 60 Hares, as well as wild Duck and Rabbits, should be got. By putting down birds, and careful management, the Shooting could be greatly improved.

Fishing – The Cruden Burn, which traverses the Estate for a distance of about two miles, affords good Trout Fishing, and in spring and autumn capital Sea Trout Fishing is obtained in the Stream which passes through the Gardens.

Net Fishing – The Net Salmon Fishing in Cruden Bay is at present let to Mr John Hector, Aberdeen, under a lease expiring at Martinmas, 1923, at a rental of £620 per annum.

Golf – See page 4. The Links are on the Estate, and are about fifteen minutes' walk from the Castle.

FEUING

A number of Feus have been given off in Port Erroll Village. Good schemes for Water Supply and Drainage have already been installed in the Village, and owing to the excellence of the Golf Links, the dry and bracing climate, and the beauty of the coast scenery, the demand for Feus is likely to increase.

HOUSE PROPERTY

There are several houses in Port Erroll Village of more or less modern construction and in good repair.

A newspaper report on 24 April, 1925, of the sale of the castle and its contents gives us some idea of how the castle looked when the Erroll family lived there.

SLAINS CASTLE SALE
Purchaser of famous 'Wishing Stone'

The sale of the furnishings of Slains Castle was concluded on Thursday, when the furniture in the bedrooms and some other effects, including the famous Wishing Stone, were disposed of by public auction. Princess Maud and Lord Carnegie were prominent amongst the buyers. It was rumoured that Lord Carnegie had purchased the castle for a place of residence, but when his lordship was interrogated by our representative he stated that there was no truth in the report.

More were present at the sale on the second day than on the first, the disposal of the bedroom furniture having a great interest among local people. The furniture was sold in the bedrooms, and great crushes were the order of the day. Most of the goods put up for auction were very ordinary, but trade was good, and although certain articles went cheap, many others fetched full value.

The 'sensation' of the day centred upon an oil painting, 'The South-West Prospect of the Seat of Colonel Geo. Boyd at Portsmouth, New Hampshire, 1774'. Hung in a plain gilt frame in a bedroom corridor, this picture had attraction only for a south firm of dealers and a private buyer. The name of the artist was unknown, but apparently value was placed upon the canvas, for, starting at £5, the bidding between the two parties mentioned rose almost unhesitatingly by 10s increases until the picture was knocked down to the private buyer for £42.

Interviewed later, the purchaser said he had no proper conception of the value of the picture, but he was of opinion that it would attract interest in the United States and his intention was to send it to New York.

The famous Wishing Stone, removed from Old Slains Castle, was purchased by Mr James Cruickshank, Kilmarnock Arms Hotel, Cruden Bay, for £7. The old Spanish cannon, of which there were four, sold – one at £2 5s, and the others at £2 15s.

Chests of drawers made up to £10, and antique mahogany poster

Slains Castle as it was when the Hays of Erroll lived there

bedsteads up to £15. An antique grandfather clock, by Alex Sangster, Cruden, made £14; a Turkey carpet, £12; an oak six-door glazed bookcase with breakfront and carved canopy, £9; an oak knee-hole dressing table with pedestals and swing glass, £8; an antique inlaid mahogany knee-hole dressing table, £7 15s; carved walnut window table, £6 5s; walnut and marqueterie inlaid commode, £7 5s; two carved antique walnut hall chairs with Renaissance backs, £7; and an antique mahogany half-circle inlaid table, £5 15s.

It was learned that the rare old Italian Renaissance blackwood cabinet of drawers, which had not found a purchaser at the first day's sale, had changed hands by private bargain.

Slains Castle as it is today

This report also informs us that:

The Erroll family had possessed an ancient pewter basin of Pictish origin; the skeleton of a primeval ox-head found in the Teuchan Moss; the eight of diamonds, on which, as a secret missive (according to one story), the Duke of Hamilton made a last effort to save the life of the Earl of Kilmarnock after Culloden; the caparisoned saddle on which Lord Fitzclarence rode to the coronation of William IV; the set of china prepared by the nation for presentation to Lord Nelson, with a portrait of Lady Hamilton in a different attitude on each of 600 pieces (this was sold in London piece by piece a good many years ago); besides a number of portraits by Vandyk, Jamesone and Sir Joshua Reynolds. The library also was worthy of note, being a fine room, fitted with oak bookcases and containing over 4,000 volumes. This library was sold to Glasgow University a number of years ago.

As for Cruden Bay's other significant building – the Cruden Bay Hotel – its days were also numbered. New holidaying fashions had appeared, and the stories of both hotel and railway faltered financially for some time. It has been said they never really paid their way. When the Second World War broke out, the Cruden Bay Hotel was taken over by the army. It was handed back in 1945, advertised for sale, but nobody would buy. In 1947 it was sold to a demolition contractor, and it was demolished in 1952–53.

The railway station went on fire on 23 April, 1931. Only the ticket stocks were saved. There were no more passenger services after October 1932. From then there were only goods trains and Cruden Bay's railway service ceased altogether in November 1945. Cruden Bay's heyday as 'The Brighton of Aberdeenshire' was over.

When I wrote *Six Buchan Villages* in 1976, I described what had occurred since the 1940s to that time. The quietness of this period was shattered, however, during the time I was writing. Then the first great pipe-line from the oil-fields of the North Sea was brought ashore at the far end of the two and half-mile crescent of sands. This installation started in May 1973.

Not a scar was left where the sands and the grassy hill-side above them were torn asunder to receive the ponderous, probing pipe, but its effects, like disseminating spores emanating from a buried yet active presence, shot up all round us.

Helicopters snarled across the skies, ferrying crews to and from the distant oil-rigs; huge pipe-laying barges, overgrown with clutters of housing and machinery, and sprouting skywards gigantic cranes, were chivvied over the sea by swarms of long-tailed tug-boats. Within the village boundaries, green fields became muddy wastes as heavy, yellow diggers delved down for foundations for hundreds of houses. A new, bigger school was promised.

Apart from these activities, life in Cruden Bay continued much the same. In the 1950s and 60s, Cruden Bay had a community club with more than 80 senior members as well as a junior section with 36 members. There were also clubs for young people and for young farmers. There were classes in dressmaking, drama, Scottish Country Dancing, benchwork, leatherwork, physical instruction and other crafts. When I wrote in 1976, on winter evenings the Drama Club rehearsed for its end-of-year production; badminton tournaments were played; the SWRI met; bowlers, golfers and farmers held their annual dinner/dances.

Perhaps most important of all, the Cruden Bay Community Association kept a watchful eye not only on village affairs, but on the powerful British Petroleum. This lively association instigated a senior Citizens' Club for the elderly and, for the young, investigated the peculiar ways of planners who sanctioned the building of a large private and a council housing estate, but 'hesitated' to provide a bigger school.

On summer days, the car park filled up and day trippers pattered across to the beach by the wooden 'Ladies' Bridge' – so called because the ladies of the village raised funds for its erection in 1923. Longer-staying visitors based at the two hotels – The Red House and the Kilmarnock Arms, and migratory cottage owners swelled the numbers. Then the four general merchants' shops, the chemist's, the butcher's, the ironmonger's, the bank and the post office enjoyed a bustle of business. A few small pleasure boats supplemented the two salmon cobbles and one remaining fishing boat at the harbour.

The period between then and now has not been as peaceful as the preceding one, especially quite recently. There have been two notable conflagrations – that of the Bowling Club's pavilion in 1997 and of Port Erroll Primary School in April 2000. This big, new school had only been opened in 1978. A temporary wooden building was erected to accommodate the children until 2003 when the present Port Erroll Primary School was opened. A new home for the Bowling Club appeared in the village's playpark in 2000, and a sports pavilion in 2002. The Cruden Bay Football team moved from the playpark to a pitch in a field at the opposite end of the village. Tennis is now played in the playpark. A library was opened early in 1989. A new golf clubhouse was opened in 1998 and a new police station came into operation in 2001. The Brickworks closed in 1990. This was the third brickworks. The first one, situated near to what is now the garage, disappeared under sand in 1881. A second one, started in 1882 to the north east of the golf clubhouse, was succeeded by this third and last manifestation in 1902 at the north end of the village.

The cost of the new golf clubhouse necessitated the Golf Club selling land for the building of what might be described as a new hamlet at the village's south boundary. The disputed 1976 housing plans referred to above resulted in the building firm of Barratts creating a new estate of private houses at the north end of the village, while at the south end an estate of wooden council houses sprang up. A complex of sheltered housing for the elderly opened in November, 1984, and a nursing home was opened on 10 February, 1990. A new surgery for the local medical practice had its official opening on 30 December, 1993. Recently, a new sewage system was installed for the village. Checking from a list in the library, I found that in Cruden Bay there are Boys' Brigade, Girl Guides, Brownies, Rainbows and Tennis Clubs, Cruden Bay Playgroup, the Cruden Bay Horticultural Society, Red Cross, Errollston Riding Stables, an Over-50 Club, SWRI, and Junior and Senior Football Clubs.

There are now two general merchants, the post office, the chemist, one joinery, the bank, one public house and three hotels.

The first Cruden Bay Brickworks, which was smothered by sand

At the end of Main Street stands a rough hewn pillar of pink granite on a circular stone base. This is a monument commemorating a historic event of nearly 90 years ago.

In the morning of Thursday 30 July, 1914, a small Bleriot monoplane called *Ca Flotte*, stood on the flat sands at Cruden Bay. It was equipped with an 80hp Gnome engine and, being a land aircraft, had landing wheels. In its body were air cushions which would keep it afloat for 24 hours should it, by some mischance, land in the sea – for it was to attempt to fly from Cruden Bay to Stavanger in Norway, and so make the first flight across the North Sea.

A crowd had gathered on Cruden Bay beach on this unusual and historic occasion. Among them were reporters and, thanks to their eye-witness accounts, we can visualise this important day for Cruden Bay. A spectator of renown was the singer, Madame Clara Butt, who at that time was holidaying in Slains Castle, and had come to give her good wishes to the young pilot, Lieutenant Trygve Gran, one time of the Norwegian Navy and one of the men who found the bodies of Captain Scott and his companions on his tragic Antarctic expedition.

This aviator, aged 26 years – a tall, handsome bachelor – had already flown the Channel, looped the loop, and climbed Mount Erebus and Mount Cook. He had also flown extensively in France. Taking his record of past courageous adventure into account, his decision to fly over the North Sea was very much in character.

Lieutenant Gran's intentions were published in the *Peterhead Sentinel* on 20 June, 1914. 'I shall start from Peterhead, thirty miles north of Aberdeen, as soon as a day comes when the weather looks fair and settled, and make for Stavanger on the west coast of Norway. I know the shores there well,' he is quoted as saying.

He went on to tell of the uncertainties connected with this challenging feat. He hoped to land on a wide sandy beach, but took into account that this might not be the case. He was taking red rockets with him in case he landed in the sea, and took comfort in the fact that many steamships plied between Peterhead and Stavanger and, consequently, he would stand a good chance of being rescued.

He was carrying enough petrol to last seven hours, which he knew to be plenty to take him the five to six hour journey to Norway. 'If I get

Lieutenant Trygve Gran's aeroplane on the sands at Cruden Bay

carried south by wind I shall have to reach the coast of Denmark which is much further, and I doubt if I shall have enough petrol for that,' he admitted.

He was not going to fly with the help of maps. 'I shall have just a piece of the Norwegian coast in front of me,' he said. As he flew, he hoped to keep a diary.

Lieutenant Gran's monoplane arrived in Cruden Bay on 17 July, 1914, but he had to wait till the 30th before weather conditions both in Scotland and Norway were favourable.

At last the right day dawned. The monoplane, sporting the figure of a small red devil as mascot on its bow, was wheeled out on the flat tawny sands. A woman in the crowd stepped out to the front of the aeroplane and added a Scottish thistle to the devil. Lieutenant Gran put into his pockets two feeding bottles with rubber tubes attached to connect them to his mouth, made one last careful inspection of his plane and climbed aboard at 8am. Five minutes later he started the engine. It sped over the sand for about 50 yards, rose at a gentle angle into the air to about 200ft., flew round the Cruden Bay Hotel where he and his team of mechanics had lodged while waiting for fair weather and then, near the Bullers o' Buchan, headed out to the North Sea.

However, about half an hour later back the monoplane came, and

Lieutenant Gran explained that about 40 miles off the coast lay dense, black fog that prevented his seeing his compass clearly, and so he had had to turn back.

It was not till 1pm that reports reached him that the fog had cleared and he was able to set off once again. This time he flew over Slains Castle at a height of about a hundred feet above the roof and soon disappeared from sight.

That night a telegram arrived in Aberdeen saying that Lieutenant Gran had landed at Stavanger about 6.30pm. The flight of 305 miles had taken him 4 hours and 10 minutes in the air.

On 27 June, 1971, a ceremony took place opposite our house on Main Street, Cruden Bay, when Major Gran, aged 83, returned with his wife and son to unveil the monument set up by pupils of Gordon's College, Aberdeen, to commemorate his pioneer flight of 1914. Trygve Gran DFC had been a major in the Royal Flying Corps and now, to acknowledge his service in it, and to honour his great achievement in 1914, Group Captain William Kelly made an appreciative speech. With the Group Captain was a contingent of Air Force personnel from RAF Buchan. Officers and cadets of the Turriff and Peterhead Air Training

Trygve Gran Memorial, at the end of Main Street, Cruden Bay

Corps also attended the ceremony with the Peterhead Salvation Army Band providing rousing music. We had heard that there was to be a fly past, but this did not occur.

Major Gran spoke at the ceremony. He recalled that a crowd, such as that on this occasion, had gathered to see his departure on 30 July, 1914, and he quoted the last words he had heard as he had climbed into his cockpit. One of the onlookers had said, 'God help that young man.'

The flight could be said to have been foreseen by Lord Kilmarnock at the celebratory dinner given for his coming of age in 1897.

> But there is a coincidence which I should like to point out – namely, that the harbour was completed in the year of my father's majority, and the railway has been completed in mine. If I may venture the conjecture, by the time a like ceremony to this is celebrated on a future occasion – [laughter] – we should at the same rate of progress witness at least the introduction of a flying machine.

We can now look back and realise how right his conjecture was. Incidentally, the harbour was completed in 1880, the railway line opened 17 years later in 1897, and 17 years after that, in 1914, Trygve Gran flew from Cruden Bay to Norway.

Happily, Main Street has remained as it was when I wrote in 1976. I can still stand at my front door and listen to Cruden Water murmuring by, the rustle of the trees on its banks and the hush of the sea on the sands of the golden beach.

CHAPTER THREE

Bullers o' Buchan

Sometime, in the dawn of history, a Blowhole came into being at the Bullers o' Buchan. The coarse, crystalline crust of earth cooled to form hard, jointed masses of pink granite. Wind and water scoured their faces and slowly, but persistently, penetrated the ragged, irregular joints. At length, the relentless waves bored out a cave, and the air that rushed in, waveborne, pressed against its roof till the weakened, jointed blocks collapsed leaving a gigantic, gaping hole in the land through which the spray from the stormy sea could blow and blast freely. The outer rim of the Blowhole, with the sea beating against its base, is a narrow, rocky strip.

From at least as early as the eighteenth-century travellers have been coming here. In 1769, Thomas Pennant visited and wrote:

> The famous Bullers o' Buchan . . . are a vast hollow in a rock, projecting into the sea, open at the top, with a communication to the sea through a noble, natural arch, through which boats can pass, and lie secure in this natural harbour. There is a path round the top, but in some parts too narrow to walk on with satisfaction, as the depth is about thirty fathom, with water on both sides, being bounded on the North and South by small creeks.

We have another first-hand report of a visit to the Bullers four years after Pennant's account. After dinner in Slains Castle on Tuesday, 24 August, 1773, Dr Samuel Johnson and James Boswell climbed into the coach ordered by the Countess of Erroll to take them to view two places of interest along the coast.

The first 'curiosity' was the rock of Dunbuy which, according to Dr Johnson, meant the Yellow Rock, so called because it was covered with sea-birds, and their droppings coloured it yellow. Pennant discovered that young kittiwakes were often eaten as an aperitif.

The second place of interest, considerably more impressive, was the Bullers o' Buchan, called locally 'the Pot'. Mr Boyd, who had entertained them in the castle, explained the word 'Buller'. He said that it came from the French *bouloir*, meaning 'to boil'. Boswell thought a simpler explanation was that it came from our own word 'boiler'.

Both visitors were greatly impressed by the phenomenon. To Boswell it was 'a monstrous cauldron'. To Johnson it looked like 'a vast well bordered with a wall' – 'He that ventures to look downward sees, that if his foot should slip, he must fall from his dreadful elevation upon stones on one side, or into the water on the other.' They walked round the abyss. Not satisfied with this venture, Johnson insisted they take a boat and go into the Pot. He described the experience:

> The bason in which we floated was nearly circular, perhaps thirty yards in diameter. We were inclosed by a natural wall, rising steep on every side to a height which produced the idea of insurmountable confinement. The interception of all lateral light caused a dismal gloom. Round us was a perpendicular rock, above us the distant sky, and below an unknown profundity of water. If I had any malice against a walking spirit, instead of laying him in the Red Sea, I would condemn him to reside in the Buller of Buchan.

Boswell found the walk round the narrow edge rather nerve-wracking – 'it alarmed me to see Dr Johnson striding irregularly along'. He noted more mundane details of the trip than did his companion. About the boatmen who took them into the Pot, he remarked: 'The Buchan men all shewing their teeth, and speaking with that strange sharp accent which distinguishes them, was to me a matter of curiosity.' Speaking of the caves inside the pot, he wrote: 'Mr Boyd told us that it is customary for the company at Peterhead well to make parties, and come and dine in one of the caves here.'

The adventure over, the coach returned them to Slains Castle where coffee and tea was waiting for them in the drawing room, which was decorated with 'a number of fine prints, and with a whole length picture of Lord Errol by Sir Joshua Reynolds'.

Since it is one of my aims to breathe life into the ruins of Slains Castle, I will tell how the visitors spent the remainder of the day there.

Boswell described a 'dry-walk' the Earl had had built, and said its galleries on both storeys of the castle were 'hung with Hogarth's works, and other prints'.

They sat in the library and at nine o'clock the Earl of Erroll arrived home. He had had a dinner engagement with Mr Irvine of Drum. Boswell was 'afraid he might have urged drinking', but the Earl had a large glass of port and water, and let his guests follow their own inclinations. The evening ended with his accompanying his guests to their bedrooms.

Boswell's night was not restful – 'I had a most elegant room, but there was a fire in it which blazed, and the sea, to which my windows looked, roared, and the pillows were made of the feathers of some sea-fowl, which had to me a disagreeable smell.'

In addition to these causes to keep him awake he let his imagination run riot. 'I saw in imagination, Lord Errol's father, Lord Kilmarnock, [who was beheaded on Tower Hill in 1746] and I was somewhat dreary.'

Twenty years later, in 1792, the Rev. Cock was saying that the Bullers o' Buchan was simply one of four fishing villages that between them had only eight boats. Each, when fully manned, had six men and a boy as crew, but very few at that time had complete crews, and some were 'laid up for want of men'. He does not describe 'the Pot of Bullers' Buchan' because he says it is so well known it would be superfluous to describe it.

The presence of 'the Pot' is all that Dr Pratt remarked on when he visited the Bullers in 1858, and James Dalgarno, the writer of *From the Brig o' Balgownie to Bullers o' Buchan*, mentioned little more when he wrote in 1896. It would seem that the Buller has been the village's claim to fame through the years.

Like everyone else, I wrote of 'the Pot' when I visited the village in 1975–76. On that visit, I recorded how I couldn't bear to watch a young woman who stepped out smartly on the narrowest bit of the rim, and then stood gazing about her, 150ft or so above the sea. Mrs Lawson, who had lived beside 'the Pot' since a child, said she often watched in trepidation the bus loads of tourists, often including children, totter round the rough, bumpy track. I asked her if she did not fear for the safety of her own little son, but he, trained since infancy never to venture near the cliffs or chasm, obeyed the rules faithfully, and caused no anxiety. The same applied to the only other two children of the village, but such rules were not always laid down in the Bullers. Mrs Philips, who used to live near Mrs Lawson, told me that the boys of the village used to cycle round 'the pot'. Another lady was of the opinion that when they came to the narrowest part of the rim they did not cycle but crossed a-straddle the rocky ridge. There is an old story that a drunken horseman once took a wager that he would gallop round. This he did successfully, but on becoming sober and aware of the risk he had taken, died of fright.

Personally I would be more inclined to follow Lord Portarlington's example. He could not bring himself to walk along even the cliff-edge path on the landward side towards 'the pot', and usually climbed over the fence and proceeded through a field.

On one occasion, having escorted a lady from the palatial Cruden Bay Hotel to introduce her to 'the Buller', he requested a little village girl to walk between him and the cliff-edge. On reaching 'the pot', the octogenarian lady, Mrs Robertson, who was that little girl, told me, 'his lordship got down on his belly, and peered over the edge.' Not even her presence could bring him to make the return journey. Lady companion or no, he clambered over the fence as was his custom. The little girl's mother had watched their progress in tears as with every 'steeter' of his lordship, she feared her daughter's disappearance over the cliff.

Despite this incident, Mrs Robertson said with a smile, 'I liked him,' and to make sure I did not dismiss him as a coward, she told me how one stormy day he insisted, against the boatman's advice, on being taken out on the rough sea. The boat nearly turned turtle and they were forced to retreat, but Lord Portarlington showed no fear, and helped to haul the boat up the beach. She also told me of the occasion when this same gentleman supped up her plate of the then novel dessert, 'Creamola', which he professed to enjoy greatly and protested he'd never tasted before 'not even at the hotel'.

Mrs Robertson could recall people picnicking on an enormous stone beached in 'the pot,' but not in the caves.

Her father, in order to be at home to care for his family, their mother being an invalid, made his living by running his trim, white-painted boat – proudly bearing in gold letters its name, *Slains Castle* – as a pleasure boat in the summer. Mrs Robertson claimed that parties from the Earl of Erroll's Castle nearly kept him fully occupied. The only well-known name she could recall was that of Prime Minister Asquith.

The boat would sail round to the Castle for the Earl and Countess and their guests, and then, having conveyed them to the Bullers and probably into 'the Pot', the boatman would unload and carry their picnic things to the nearby cliff-tops.

On 20 October, 1897, the boatman from the Bullers was called upon to act in a completely different capacity. This was the evening on which a ball was held at Slains Castle to celebrate the majority of the eldest son, Lord Kilmarnock, and the boatman was invited to the ball and asked to officiate as floor-master. The countess pinned on his breast a red and grey rosette decorated with a 'K' in silver cord and two silver cord tassels. His daughter still kept this memento which, for the years of her childhood, she insisted on pinning to whatever garment she was wearing.

Mrs Cruickshank, a friend in my own village of Cruden Bay, and who as a child visited almost daily her grandparents at the Bullers, remembered being told how, at certain seasons, a coach and footman would come from Slains Castle to take her mother there to mend the linen. As a girl, her mother had a reputation for fine needlework. Mrs Cruickshank could herself remember parties from the Cruden Bay Hotel and the Kilmarnock Arms, Cruden Bay, arriving by waggonette, and the local children running excitedly alongside for the scattering of pennies by the gentry.

There was a spring at the foot of the rocks at the Bullers said to be 'full as strong a mineral as that of Peterhead'. Perhaps this was an added attraction. If it tasted as good as the crystal-clear ice-cold

Bullers o' Buchan as it is today. The top of the 'pot' can be seen to the right

glassful Scott Lawson kindly brought me from the open well on the cliff-side at the Bullers, it would have been worth the visit. Mrs Pinn, an attractive Peterhead girl married to a soft-voiced young American from the Rocky Mountains, explained to me how, turn about with the other three women of the village, she took her special scrubbing brush, let the well drain itself and scrubbed clean the rocky cavity. Mrs Lawson told how they used to keep a little eel in the well to scavenge, but one newcomer, taking a turn at scrubbing and not understanding the poor creature's function, dispatched it. A mains supply was now available throughout the village, but everybody, even in the 1970s, seemed to be sticking to their centrifugal pump and the well. Mrs Buchan, the senior citizen, said in a rather defensive tone when I mentioned the mains supply – 'We have *spring* water.' Four cottages were about to be renovated and when I visited I wondered what the coming inhabitants would choose to do.

In the days of rail in this area a siding was made at the Bullers. Mr Burnett, retired near the village, told me how as a child he was taken first by horse-drawn bus from Peterhead to Boddam and thence by train to Cruden Bay from where the family walked to the Bullers and had tea in the tea-room at the back of cottage Number 1. Then they travelled out to 'the Buller's Halt' to stop a homeward bound train with the wave of a hand. Mr Burnett expressed concern that in this day and age nothing had really been done by the powers that be to provide for the needs of tourists coming to the Bullers. There were no public conveniences or litter bins, and despite recent re-alignment of the road to create a fairly commodious lay-by, only a solitary litter bin has been provided.

Sometimes as many as eight bus-loads a day would stop at the Bullers. Mrs Lawson's cottage was right on the front corner by which all had to pass to 'the Pot'. She found it interesting, at times amusing, to see the various fashions sported, and quite enjoyed snippets of conversation with Australians, New Zealanders, Swiss and so on. I asked the four households if they minded the constant influx of people throughout the summer, but they all seemed to accept the situation with equanimity.

Mrs Buchan wisely took advantage of the position and had established a shell-craft industry in the front room of 'Tugela,' the only house in the village with a name and that taken from a river in Natal. Jar upon jar of carefully cleaned and graded shells waited to change bottles into exotic lamps and create all sorts of decorative knick-knacks. Mrs Buchan, sometimes accompanied by grandchildren, made pilgrimages to surrounding beaches to collect her shells.

Within living memory, apart from one fishing boat, tourism seems to have been the sole industry at the Bullers.

From the statistical tables giving the Creek Returns for the East Coast of Scotland in 1855, we see that there were three boats of 30ft upwards, six measuring 28ft–30ft, and five under 18ft at the Bullers o' Buchan. Quite an improvement since Alexander Cock recorded the state of affairs in 1792, when Bullers o' Buchan shared eight boats with Longhaven, Ward and Whinnyfold. In 1855, the Bullers' 14 boats were manned by 30 fishermen and boys, and the fishing industry was executed by 30 gutters and packers, 48 vendors and makers of nets and one curer. Even so, in 1875, 'There are three white-fishing stations and boat-landing places: one at Whinnyfold, one at Ward of Cruden and one at Bullers o' Buchan, but most of the boats, however, land at the two former places.'

The fishing story follows the same pattern as that of all the Buchan villages. In 1881, there were 21 boats and 42 fishermen. In 1928, only one sailing boat and two fishermen were left.

Mrs Philips recalled that 66 years ago there were three sailing boats. The dozen houses were all inhabited, but the menfolk earned their livelihoods at the granite quarry of Longhaven, on the railway, at the brickworks in Cruden Bay, and one was Caddy Master at the Cruden Bay golf course.

I wrote in 1976 that, of the three men, two were long-distance lorry drivers, and one, the young man from America, was in our latest North-east industry – the oil.

The children were transported to school. In the past, the scholars from the Bullers walked about two miles to Longhaven, barefoot in summer, tackety boots amidst the wreaths of snow in the winter, carrying their pieces to have with soup made at the school.

On Friday evenings the young people assembled in the empty 'room end' of the shop to dance to the melodeon, and on Sunday morning might walk about two miles as far as 'the Chapel' – the Episcopal St James the Less, on the hill beyond Cruden Bay. In the afternoon they might attend Sunday School in the Mission Hall in the tiny next-door hamlet of North Haven.

Mrs Cruickshank recalled the evening when the entire population gathered to enjoy the first gramophone – the kind with cylinders and horn. One of the village boys had been loaned it from the Professional Golfer at Cruden Bay.

These entertainments helped the dark, winter nights to pass, nights when 'the pot' boiled as it must have done on 18 January, 1912.

That night distress flares lit the sky above the Bullers and Mrs Robertson's father sent one of his sons for the rocket brigade. The *Wistow Hall*, a steamer of Liverpool, had been driven ashore. Another of Mrs Robertson's brothers made his way down the cliffs to reach a man swept up on the rocks below. He took the lascar, who asked fearfully, 'You – my friend?' on his back, and clambered back to safety.

The seaman would not part with his rescuer's cap, but kept it beside him under his bedclothes, displaying it to all who visited, and explaining: 'He was the one who rescued me.' Fifty-three lives were lost that night; four were saved.

One stormy night shortly before my visit, when the thunder bellowed overhead, Mrs Pinn's phone rang. It was Mrs Lawson who, knowing her neighbour was alone that night, suggested she might like to come over to her cottage for company. At that time nobody at the Bullers felt isolated. A telephone call would bring immediate help from any of the four, snug cottages.

There seemed to be many pleasant facets to life at the Bullers. On the practical side, the butcher, the baker, the fishmonger and the grocer came with their vans every week.

The other day I spoke to one of the three children whom I had met on my visit to the village in the 1970s. Now a pleasant young woman, Veronica Smith brought me up-to-date with the village's story, and I'm glad to say there has not been radical change in the interval.

There are now nine occupied houses, into one of which – her family home – Veronica has returned to live. Many, I noticed, have extensions, and all looked snug and trim. The population is now twelve. Two of the inhabitants are retired, but most have jobs: some in computers and some in the oil industry. There is only one child who travels by school bus to Longhaven School.

The well water which I sampled all those years ago is no longer used. Having it regularly tested proved quite expensive. The many vans which called previously no longer operate, and people shop in Peterhead and Aberdeen. I noticed several cars and garages.

One boat lay under wraps near a house and on the beach there was a kayak. The boat owner goes fishing occasionally when he returns home from working abroad. The only boats that Veronica had seen in 'the pot' were fishing boats setting, or hauling, lobster creels.

Veronica thought the eight bus-loads of tourists per day in Mrs Lawson's time had decreased. I asked if any tourists ventured round 'the pot' and she said she'd seen some proceed along the narrow rim on hands and knees. People nowadays usually picnic near the car park on the edge of the village, and children are not frequently brought in to walk near cliffs and chasm. A litter bin has been provided in the car park, but still a much needed public convenience and telephone kiosk are required. In time of emergencies – and people do fall over the cliffs from time to time – there's sometimes difficulty in finding an available phone.

Good neighbourliness is still in force. When a pet dog fell over the cliffs, Veronica's father and another village neighbour climbed down and rescued it, and it survives to this day.

My husband and I walked through the village almost to 'the pot' along a path bordered by a grassy bank bright with sea-pinks, purple vetch and glowing yellow birds-foot-trefoil on one side and, on the other, by cliffs over which fulmar petrels swooped, where sea-pinks nodded in the breeze and from which rose the chatter of nesting kittiwakes – the only sound except for the occasional bark of a dog that broke the silence enveloping the little village that Sunday morning.

I can still agree with Veronica when she said that she liked the Bullers o' Buchan because it was such a peaceful place.

CHAPTER FOUR

Whinnyfold

On summer afternoons in the nineteenth century, guests, residing in the palatial Cruden Bay Hotel, could be seen strolling across the sandy beach to the small village of Whinnyfold on the cliff-tops about three miles to the south of Cruden Bay. They were going to have afternoon tea in some of the cottages. They would have met very few villagers, for summer days brought the shoals of herrings off the north-east coast of Scotland, and the Whinnyfold folk closed their houses, and rented accommodation in Peterhead for the herring fishing season.

However, one lady had to stay behind to care for an aged mother, and this enterprising daughter moved into her wash-house, and used her house and those of several absent relatives as a series of tea-rooms. The fare was boiled eggs and home-baked scones, and she had plenty of customers. One guest who came and stayed in her house, called

Old Whinnyfold

'Crookit Lum' because of its crooked chimney, was Bram Stoker – manager of the famous actor, Sir Henry Irving, and writer of *Dracula*, and, more importantly when speaking of Whinnyfold, *The Mystery of the Sea*. From his tale we can imagine him clambering about the steep cliffs, venturing into the dark, dank caves, gazing at the cruel fangs of the rocks called the 'Skares' and being inspired by the wild, storm-blasted setting. I spoke to the niece of his hostess, a Mrs Taylor. She herself was a septuagenarian when I interviewed her but remembered how she had, when a girl, assisted her aunt as a tablemaid. I asked if she could recall the names of any of the titled and wealthy who came from the Cruden Bay Hotel, but the only people she could remember by name were Sir Jeremiah and Lady Colman.

When the Whinnyfold folk were at home, sandy, gritty lug worms, sore on the women's fingers as they baited the 'small' lines, arrived from as far away as Ardersier on the west coast, and from the River Ythan at Newburgh. Lug worms are a kind of sand worm and they were attached to the small hooks of the 'small' fishing lines used for catching haddock and whiting. 'Great' lines had larger hooks for catching larger fish such as cod and skate.

Hard, shiny mussels – bivalve molluscs – came by the lorryload from the River Ythan at Newburgh. The fisherfolk carried them down the almost vertical cliff-face in their creels and 'planted' them out on bare flat rocks in beds, which they called 'scabs'. Then, when the seawater washed over them, the creatures anchored themselves down and provided a living supply of bait for days at a time. The women carried the mussels up the cliff as they were needed and deftly prised them open with their 'sheil blades' – knives sharpened on both sides. A mussel shell or a teaspoon were the tools for scooping out limpets, another important source of bait, when they were brought from the rocks on the home shore.

Mrs Taylor remembered how on one occasion some fishermen calling by a woman busy at her washing, mentioned that their particular 'scabs' were empty of mussels. She stopped her washing and, as generations of Whinnyfold women had done before her, hoisted her creel over her shoulders, and immediately set off to the mussel beds by the Ythan – about eight or nine miles distant.

A typical cottage in Old Whinnyfold

Within living memory, fisherwomen set off from Whinnyfold in the dark of the morning, flickering lanterns in their workworn hands and creels heavy with fish on their backs. They walked 12 or so miles to Peterhead, and then walked all the way back home at the end of a day of selling fish.

But Whinnyfold fish went much further afield and won wide acclaim. In Edinburgh there once hung a sign 'The Real Johnny Gray', advertising haddocks smoked in a fish kiln in Old Whinnyfold – the original village barely half a mile to the landward of the New Village built on the cliff-tops.

Women gutted, washed and packed mackerel, sometimes till midnight. Lobsters were hauled from a sheltered pool north of 'Gaudman's Rock' where they were stored in boxes and Mr Parley came with his horse and cart from his little croft nearby, collected the produce of Whinnyfold, and trundled it away to Cruden Bay railway station. Manchester was one market, and many an anxiously awaited telegram was dispatched from that great, distant city to the villagers on the cliffs, telling them what price their fish had fetched.

Whitings – split, salted and hung to dry on the fencing wires – were, when preserved, threaded into bundles on dried rushes and bought by visitors who sometimes came specially to obtain this delicacy.

When winter storms threatened, the women pushed the capstans round with all their might to help their menfolk haul the boats high off the beach. Then there was no fish to bring home any money and times were hard. One mother told her children in later years how once, when she had not a penny in the house, she went outside and came upon a sixpence. She suspected that someone, knowing of her plight, had left it for her to find.

She would then have been able to make her way up the road to Old Whinnyfold and Mary Taylor's shop where almost anything could be purchased. Mary Taylor was remembered for her calm, uncomplaining nature. The young people of the village and surrounding countryside congregated nightly in her low, thatched cottage – often even the beds were used as seating accommodation – and no matter what high jinks ensued, Mary tolerated all.

On occasion a store for nets came in handy for a dance of sorts and other more active forms of jollification. Some of the farm-working boys from round about would add to the gaiety with music from their melodeons.

New Whinnyfold when still a busy fishing village

Such happy times at home could only be enjoyed for part of the year. About March, some of the fishermen went to the 'great lines' off Shetland. Then came the tenth day in May and it was time to catch herrings off the north-east coast and process them in Peterhead. From the end of August and through September there was a lull in which nets were repaired. From 10 October till late November the shoals were churning up the sand off Lowestoft and Yarmouth.

In 1855, there were 58 fishermen in Whinnyfold and 183 people employed in the fishing industry. They had 24 boats including three large drifters for herring fishing. This situation was still very much the same 30 years later, but then the village began to feel the effects of change in fishing methods with which they tried in vain to compete.

By 1928, according to a newspaper report, there were only four boats sailing from the village – 'half the fleet that had been at the beginning of the century'. It cost them 4/- to send one to four boxes to Cruden Bay station, and their earnings were only 10/- or 12/- per box. Fisherwomen were no longer prepared to hawk the produce round the country. They had no harbour. But, more damaging than any of these disadvantages, were the operations of the trawlers. They simply plundered the seas, leaving next to nothing for the smaller boats.

However, both the writer in the newspaper and Peter Anson, who wrote about the village in 1929, remarked that the village of Whinnyfold 'is one of the most energetic to be found along the coast'.

A year before Peter Anson's visit, the first motor boat had been introduced. He found 19 fishermen, whom he described as 'among the most successful great line fishermen on the east coast of Scotland'. They also owned two steam drifters based in Peterhead. At that time, they were not only reluctant to pull up their roots and move elsewhere because of ties of birth, kinship and home, but they were aware that they would most likely find no buyers for their houses.

Eventually, however, the Whinnyfold folk did have to leave. When I visited in the 1970s there were only nine of the original inhabitants of the village. People from many different places had happily settled beside them. There was a population of 28.

No children in tackety boots and moleskin trousers trudged the two miles to the Erroll Schools – so called because the single building was divided into a boys' school and a girls' school – in Cruden Bay. Whinnyfold's four scholars were transported to the new Port Erroll School, Cruden Bay, by school bus or, for secondary education, to Peterhead Academy by public bus.

There was no 'Mary Taylor' of any kind. Where ten cottages, including her shop and one other like it, had made up Old Whinnyfold, there was now one little house in ruins and several grassy humps.

Three butcher vans came, there was a baker's van twice a week, a fishmonger brought some fruit and groceries with him, and milk was delivered every second day. To obtain any other requirements the inhabitants had either to use their own transport or take the morning bus to Peterhead via Cruden Bay, and return by one of two that came southwards in the late afternoon. Today, the population totals 26 (18 adults and eight children). Seven of the children have been here since birth but only one man is a native of Whinnyfold and one other man was brought up in the village. The children of school age travel by school bus to Port Erroll Primary School or Peterhead Academy. A van, selling fish and other items calls once a week. Milk is still delivered three times a week and now the mobile library calls once a fortnight. A derelict house, now bought and being restored, was cleaned out and used for the village's Burns Supper and for the celebrations on Bonfire Night.

Mr Tom Hay, a Whinnyfold man who has lived in Peterhead for many years, but still regards the village as 'home', keeps a small boat there. His boat is named *Inch Perl* after a rock a mile south of Whinnyfold. A fisherman all his life, he now catches lobsters purely for pleasure. Tom Hay said the fishermen's move away from the village had been because Peterhead's full tide harbour made their work so much easier than it was in Whinnyfold where boats had to be beached every night. Interestingly, Tom did not agree with those that blamed the demise of inshore white fishing on the advent of the trawlers. He believed the shortage of fish was the result of pollution.

Life at Whinnyfold apparently bears little resemblance to the life of its past. Even the coastguard watch-hut that used to stand on the edge of the cliff is no longer there. One wonders if its demise was wise, for dangers still lurk off Whinnyfold as they have done through the centuries. A Whinnyfold man, Mr Cay, resident in Peterhead, listed for me in the 1970s more than a dozen wrecks he had either heard of or witnessed. With his father, he had watched helpless as the *Frederick Snowdon*, a three-masted coal boat, foundered in a south easterly storm. Every man on board was drowned. Again, on a day of south easterly gale which veered to the north west and drove blinding snow across the storm-tossed sea, he had seen the *Xenia* from Denmark crash on the vicious Skares of Cruden. One life was lost that day.

Our talk ended on a happier note. Bram Stoker's landlady gave hospitality to the rescued captain of the *Xenia*. Before he took his next ship out of Aberdeen he wired her to join him, and took her home to visit his no doubt grateful family in Copenhagen. Eventually, it was another shipwreck which brought romance into the life of this lady. The captain of a vessel which came to salvage a ship fell in love with her. They were married and, as all the best stories end, lived happily ever after.

CHAPTER FIVE

Collieston

One night in 1631 a solemn torch-lit procession made its way from Slains Castle, on the cliff-tops to the north of Cruden Bay, to St Ternan's Church in the village of Collieston, a distance of about eight miles. It was the funeral procession of Francis, 9th Earl of Erroll, and its destination was the Errolls' Aisle in St Ternan's Church. Earl Francis had stipulated that his funeral be simple and that the money, which might have been spent on a grand funeral, be given to the poor.

My husband and I visited the old aisle – the only part of the original St Ternan's Church which was replaced by the present building in 1806. There was only one tombstone in the aisle: a dark, prostrate one. We could only make out a word here and there, but the word 'argent' – meaning silver – convinced us that we were standing by the grave of Lady Mary Hay, 14th in the Erroll line, and of her husband Alexander Hay, 'who desired to be buried side by side', having 'lived in wedlock peacefully and lovingly for twenty-seven years'. They had also wanted inscribed on their gravestone the fact that no silver, gold or treasure had been interred with them. Could this have been a way of ensuring that their last resting place would be left undisturbed?

Another grave we visited in St Ternan's Churchyard, because of the tragic story associated with it, was that of Philip Kennedy, which was situated near the gate. Again the scene was set in Collieston at night. The date was 19 December, 1798, and Philip Kennedy, a young man of 38 years, was out on the road, one of a band of smugglers bringing home the night's cargo landed from a lugger in some secret creek, and hidden most probably in a cave the previous night. Philip and a few

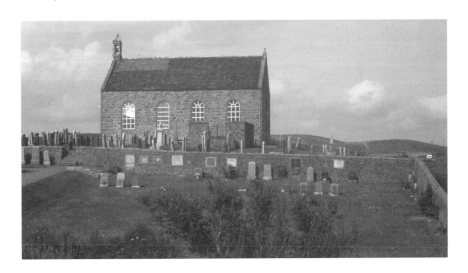

*St Ternan's Church, Collieston, with the Errolls' Aisle
(in front of the far right-hand window)*

others went ahead of the cart of booty to ensure a clear passage, but, about a quarter of a mile north of the Kirk of Slains, three excise officers blocked their way. Philip seized two of the excisemen and, holding them down, shouted to his accomplices to take hold of the third officer. But he called in vain for assistance. The other smugglers had disappeared among bushes of broom on the nearby braes. The free exciseman, Anderson, then struck Philip's head repeatedly with his sword. Still, Philip held on to his captives. Then Anderson, checking by the light of the moon that he was striking with the edge of his sword, struck a blow that split open Philip's skull. Somehow the wounded man made his way to a farm, Kirkton of Slains, nearly a quarter of a mile distant. There, on a wooden bench – a 'deis' – Philip died, his last words being, 'If all had been as true as I was, the goods would have been safe, and I should not have been bleeding to death.' The excisemen were tried in the High Court of Justiciary in Edinburgh and were acquitted of his murder. When I talked to Collieston people in the 1970s, the blood-stained deis had been presented to the Collieston Amenities Association. It is now back in the farmhouse of Kirkton of Slains where it rightly belongs.

I have read that there were two smuggling syndicates set up in Collieston, and the four luggers, two in each syndicate, were in constant use. They carried loads of salmon as far south as Folkstone and came back with their barrels full of gin. A visitor to practically any dwelling throughout the district would quite likely be offered in those days not a cup of a tea (though tea being a taxed commodity was most probably part of the contraband), but a glass of gin or brandy. Dr Lewis Mackie, a resident of the village, who has made an extensive study of the smuggling trade, told me that among goods smuggled were tobacco, lace, combs, mirrors, powder for gentlemen's wigs, bricks and tiles. Dr J. B. Pratt, writing in 1858, stated 'so little was the feeling of disgrace attached to this demoralising traffic, that there was scarcely a family along the coast, from the Don to the Spey, that was not more or less embarked in it.' Pratt then explained that the people thought of it not as smuggling, but as 'free-trading' by which they, still Jacobites at heart, were doing damage to the House of Hanover. The so-called 'free-trading' 'was exalted to the dignity of a political principle', said Pratt.

With an abundance of caves and inlets round its shores, Collieston was an ideal place for the 'free-trade' and the *Crookit Mary*, and other ships like her, were expert at appearing, signalling and slipping out of sight from land till nightfall when they quietly made their way to a suitable creek, and unloaded their illicit cargo.

Many ruses were practised to transmit secretly the arrival of a lugger, to store the contraband safely in various hide-outs till darkness fell again and, when distributed, to keep it hidden from the law. Hollow glass rolling pins and old-fashioned weather glasses were prized in Collieston as receptacles for gin and brandy. Smuggling was carried on extensively at the end of the eighteenth century and at the beginning of the nineteenth.

About the same time as smuggling was going on apace, the Rev. Alexander Farquhar, minister of Slains Parish, writing in 1791, recorded that most of the population of Collieston and Oldcastle – 146 males and 173 females – made 'their living by the sea except a trifle that the women make in winter or during stormy weather by working stockings for the Aberdeen manufacturers'.

For most of the year half the fish caught was taken by boat to Leith,

Aberdeen, Dundee or Perth, and the women carried the other half in their creels to Aberdeen and through the country to places as far away as Old Meldrum at least 15 miles distant.

It was mainly the women also who gathered the bait and carried it home in their creels three 'English' miles from the River Ythan. As the writer of the 1791 *Statistical Account* said, 'that burdensome journey made their bait dear enough, even if they paid nothing'. However, pay they did. The tacksman at the river charged them 20 shillings per year and only allowed the Collieston fisherfolk to gather from their own side of the river. This meant that they sometimes could not gather enough and had to buy more at sixpence a peck from the tacksman. The tacksman too bargained for their ling and cod caught between 1 October and 1 February. The fisherfolk could not get them dried at this time of year and so could not carry them to a better market. It was not yet their practice to barrel fish, but the tacksman did.

During the 1840s and 50s, 250 people were employed in the fishing industry. According to the 1840 *Statistical Account*, the tacksman at the Ythan, was now charging the young men £3 per year, and those over 60, £2. He allowed them to fish only twice a day to conserve his stock of mussels needed by other coastal villages as well.

Haddocks were smoked and exported to Leith and Glasgow. From the haddock fishing each man could earn, weather permitting, £1 per week. Cod was caught from October to February and a merchant pickled them for the London market at the average price of £1 and eight shillings per barrel. Each barrel contained 70 fish for which he paid the fishermen fourpence each.

Around 1840, five boats with the required crew of men and women for herring fishing had ventured to Peterhead for the season. The minister commented that the venture had turned out to be 'not so detrimental to morals as might have been expected from the accounts given of the demoralising effects of this sort of occupation'. Peter Anson wrote that in 1880 there were 64 boats and 170 fishermen in Collieston.

In 1894, a pier was built in Collieston. The fishermen had come to the conclusion that, in order to compete with other places, they required bigger boats. Bigger boats would need a sheltered harbour where they could lie afloat because their size would make it impossible to haul them up the beach as the fishermen, helped by the women, did with their present small craft at the end of each trip.

The *Aberdeen Journal* of Thursday, 18 October, 1894, reported:

Never in the quiet and happily uneventful annals of the picturesquely-situated fishing village of Collieston and district was there a more interesting or important occasion than that which marked its history yesterday, when the foundation-stone of the new harbour was laid, amid many demonstrations of enthusiasm, by Lady Gordon Cathcart of Cluny, who was accompanied by Sir R.Cathcart.

Throughout the district flags flew and at various strategic points floral arches displayed the word 'Welcome'. On one arch the fishermen had written 'Haste ye back again'. Schoolchildren had a holiday and joined a band-led procession that marched from the harbour to meet Lady Gordon Cathcart, her husband and other important guests. Such was the enthusiasm on the arrival of the Cathcarts' carriage that the fishermen unyoked the horses and pulled it to the harbour themselves, where a carpeted platform and the foundation stone draped in the Union Jack were waiting.

Lady Gordon Cathcart placed what was described as a casket containing some British and American coins, newspapers of the day and a manuscript telling of the pier project into a cavity below where the foundation stone was to be placed. The stone was lowered into position and Lady Cathcart completed the ceremony with a silver trowel and silver mallet. The celebration that followed included a boat race, a luncheon, concluded with many speeches, and a tea and presents of Bibles to the children. The entire entertainment was paid for by Sir Reginald and Lady Gordon Cathcart.

In one of the after-luncheon speeches it was suggested that a railway branch line might be run from the Great North of Scotland's Cruden Railway to the village or, failing that, a screw steamer might be obtained that would solve Collieston's fisher community's very real problem as to how to get their fish to market. Neither of those schemes were realised.

Peter Anson, writing in 1929, said that by 1900 there were only 16 boats, by 1929, 14 – none with engines – and the 12 fishermen left were well over middle age. The building of the pier had given the fishermen a haven, but it had also closed off a passage known as the North Haven through which the sea had previously flowed freely and scoured out the harbour. As a consequence, sand settled in the new harbour, silted it up and made it too shallow for the bigger steam trawlers now required and in vogue in Aberdeen. Young fishermen left to join the larger boats in Aberdeen. Families followed and settled mainly in the district of Aberdeen called Torry.

By the third *Statistical Account*, written in 1952, about half a dozen men went to the line fishing. Before the Second World War, there were only five boats fishing out of Collieston. After the War, there was only one commercial fisherman. Rear Admiral Ritchie told me his name was Norman Grant and he died in 1957. When I visited the village in the 1970s there was nobody who earned his living by fishing out of Collieston. The same is the case today. There is only recreational fishing.

Another sign of the change in emphasis in modern Collieston from that of the past has been the reducing in the 1990s of the 16 or so strong Rocket Brigade to an Initial Response Team of four men who join Cruden Bay's similar organisation for exercises in life-saving on the coast. Collieston's Rocket Brigade had a high reputation and, for their brave and successful rescues of seamen from shipwrecks, won the shield twice.

Dick Ingram, a native of Collieston in his late 60s or early 70s, told me in the 1970s that, in his day, herring boats went as far afield as Baltasound in Shetland, Stronsay in Orkney, and some even to Yarmouth. At the end of the season, they sailed up the Ythan to a piece of flat ground opposite the present farm of Waterside. When the tide was high enough they borrowed six or seven horses from the farm, and with the help of rollers dragged the boats ashore. This place was still known as the 'Herring Boats'. Dick also remembered mussels being brought home by the cart-load, and explained to me that when a fisherman worked two lines it meant he had 600 hooks to bait each time, and so mussels were needed in their thousands. The enormous quantities of empty shells became the roads of Collieston, the main one of which became known as the 'Shellie Roadie'.

In a paper by Dr Mackie, entitled *Inshore Line Fishing at Collieston*, I found the following detailed information:

Fishing was carried on of the inshore variety mostly, but also deep water fishing on what was called the 'Hard Grun' at about six fathoms.

Three types of lines were used:

Sma' line, consisting of hemp cord 3/32 of an inch thick for backing, made up of strings or hanks of 65 fathom, often referred to as 'pun-line', since it weighed out at a pound per string.

Sma'gretlin with a backing of hemp, 5/32 of an inch, used mostly for winter cod fishing and often called 'pun and a half line'.

Gretlin, for longliners, often called 'five pun line', used in deep waters such as off Iceland. This, however was never used in the inshore fishing.

Each village had its own variation in the number of hooks per string and the number of strings per line as, originally, the lines were made by the elderly men in the place. Latterly they were factory made.

In Collieston a string was 65 fathoms with a hundred hooks per string and seven strings per line.

Hooks were hung from lengths of hemp called 'snoods', which were tied to the backing by a clove hitch then two inches plaited as a stiffener with another twelve inches of single strand hemp before putting on a length of plaited horsehair spun in two strands, each with five hairs per strand. A haddock hook was then 'beat' on with linen thread to make a total length from backing to hook of 36 to 40 inches in the sma'line. The horsehair could not be used from a mare as the hair rotted easily. Fishermen preferred white hair for sandy ground and black for rocky ground. Latterly, when synthetic coraline came into use, it was shown that colour did not really matter.

However, the fishing is over and the fiddle no longer plays the 'Lang Reel o' Collieston'. It was danced at weddings and picnics for generations on a flat bit of ground at the end of the Forvie Sands. The fiddle played, the bride and bridegroom started the dance, pair after pair linked themselves into it, and then dropped off, leaving the bridal couple dancing alone at the end.

The Rev. J. Murray, in a lecture given in 1952, told of how one villager recited in verse the story of how the wedding companies used to dance all the way from the church with handkerchiefs or ribbons flying over their shoulders. Even the minister was supplied with blue ribbons.

The wedding festivities over, the bride started a life of toil. When the men set sail, the women removed their 'shore shoon' and stockings, and tucking up their skirts, 'floated' their menfolk – that is, carried them on their backs out to the floating boats. In this way, the men's feet in their long leather boots made by the local souter, and saturated with sperm oil, were kept dry for the fishing trip. The women gathered big boulders and bore them by the creelful out to the boats in which the stones were used for ballast.

A lull between seasons in the fishing perhaps meant respite from humping heavy creels of fish and bait about, but that was when the annual blanket-washing was held. Everybody's pot, tub and blankets were collected by a cart, and the womenfolk repaired to Sand Loch, kindled their fires, boiled their pots, trampled their blankets and spread them out on the bents to dry.

In 1791, the children of Collieston and Oldcastle could go to a school somewhere in the parish of Slains. If they had lessons in Latin and arithmetic they had to pay two shillings a quarter. English and writing cost one shilling and sixpence. The schoolmaster was paid six bolls, two firlots, two pecks of meal, and ten shillings and sevenpence. The Rev. Mr Alexander Farquhar said that the average number of scholars in winter was 40, but scarcely 20 attended in summer because every child aged six to seven was kept home to prepare the fishing lines.

In 1840, the Rev. James Rust recorded that two years earlier 'a very handsome schoolhouse' had been built. Seemingly, its actual construction left much to be desired for rain was, as he wrote, 'greatly damaging the roof and walls'. By this time the schoolmaster had an annual salary of £30, and reading, writing, arithmetic, Latin, mathematics and navigation were taught. In Collieston itself there was, in the 1800s, an 'adventure' school for mostly young children who were, according to Mr Rust, only taught 'the rudiments of education'. Very probably this was the establishment known as 'Geordie Tough's

Squeel' immortalised in verse in 1881 by an ex-pupil, John Walker Ritchie.

> Besides overseeing a wide and varied curriculum, Geordie
> Kent aye fat wis gweed for sairs,
> Had a kin-kind o' draps an' mixters,
> Healin' saws an' stickin' plaisters
> An' siller buckles – strange concerns –
> For curin' puir forespoken bairns.
> The educational aims were stated thus:
> Tae mak' a workin' thinkin' nation,
> Tae help a man dae better work
> In labour, commerce, State or Kirk.
> To this end the pupils were taught:
> . . . tae vreet a letter,
> An' richly train't oor han's an' min's
> Tae readin' beuks an' reddin' lines.
> Tae makin' sneeds an' keepin' coonts
> An splicin' lines an' beetin' wints.
> He sometimes made strae ropes as weel
> Tae wup a lum or thack a hoose.
> Came examination time, and Geordie called upon the village experts.
> The Minister:
> Wis maist exactin'
> In scrapin', booin' an' curtsy actin'.
> And made sure the catechism and Biblical knowledge were up to scratch.
> Merchan' Willie tried oor coontin.
> Cooper Jamie speirt oor spellins.
> And an elder called John examined the writing.

About 1900 the Bruce Hay Girls' School was closed. It had been erected and endowed in 1876 by Margaret Bruce, widow of James Hay, a fish curer in Collieston. In 1950, the last school in Collieston was closed. The village changed dramatically. Houses derelict for years were sold for the now incredible figure of about £20 and were rebuilt for summer residences, holiday lets and winter homes for young couples.

However, as early as 1930, Lawrence of Arabia, calling himself Aircraftsman Shaw, and two friends were able to rent a house for a holiday. An old gentleman sunning by his door pointed it out – a very fine, many roomed house overlooking the harbour, but assured me it bore little resemblance to the cottage of Lawrence's holiday. It had only three rooms at that time and Lawrence described it as a hovel. Most of the other houses would have been of similar size and appearance, scattered over the grassy sea-cliff that curves down to the beach.

Lawrence and his friends took reluctant turns at sweeping the floor and bringing in water and coal. They made the middle room their sitting-room, as it had a fireplace. The bed was pushed back into a corner and there, Lawrence said, he sat all day and thought while turning drying swimsuits and sucking pandrops by the pound – a sweet seemingly discovered with delight on coming to Aberdeenshire. He also read with enjoyment a history by H. G. Wells. He was anxious to obtain a book called *Novels Today* and tried to get a copy when he made a trip to Aberdeen very probably on his Brough Superior motorbike with nickel-plated twin exhausts, which Dick Ingram could remember seeing.

Those early tourists had their meals in the shop-cum-post office of that time. At some meal or other they tasted 'speldings' – haddocks caught in the morning, and split, cleaned, salted and dried by sun and wind as they hung on wood and wire netting erections by the cottage doors. They were roasted on a brick in front of the fire on the day they were caught; on subsequent days the dried fish were cooked in hot water. They were considered a great delicacy and people often came to the village to have spelding teas which were served in some of the cottages. Dick Ingram's mother used to pack her summer harvest of speldings in a white pillow-case and lay it on top of the meal in the girnal.

Rear Admiral Ritchie told me that before 1911 there had been White's hotel, but in October of that year the women of the village had appealed to the Council to close it down because their husbands gathered there on Sundays, and indulged in drinking and often fisticuffs instead of helping to prepare the fishing lines for the next day. In the 1970s, Dick Ingram told me that the same hotel, which he called

Whiteness Hotel, had been a shooting lodge and a military residence before being turned into a private house divided into three flats. For a few years there was a little cannery in what had once been the stables of the Whiteness Hotel. But the inn called The Red Lion, where the stagecoach called in the past, has disappeared completely.

Nowadays, there is no hotel or pub in the village, but a very important and active village organisation, the Collieston Amenities Committee, obtains a license and there are pub nights and pub quizzes held in the old school, now the Community Centre.

The Collieston Amenities Committee was started in 1957 by the late Sir Douglas Ritchie to be an instrument for raising funds to save the deteriorating pier, and so achieve one of its aims – 'to maintain, protect and preserve the character and amenities of the village'. Rear Admiral Steve Ritchie, son of Sir Douglas, has always played a leading and beneficial role in the life of the village. He was, until retirement, one of the Harbour Trustees responsible for upkeep of the pier. He also had a distinguished naval career and was Hydrographer to the Royal Navy from 1966–71. On retiring from the Navy, he was President of the International Hydrographic Bureau based in Monaco, and campaigned for many years for the Navy's hydrographic archive, which contains charts from the voyages of Captain Cook and earlier, to be found a suitable home. In 2002, he was invited to cut the first turf for a new building to house the archive. This building, in Taunton, Somerset, is named the Ritchie Building in his honour. Now in his late 80s, Rear Admiral Ritchie is descended from an old Collieston fisher family and so can be claimed by the village as a distinguished son.

When Rear Admiral Ritchie stayed in Monaco he learned the French game of boules, and on returning to his native village he taught others the game. In 1985, the Collieston Boules Club was established. In 1999, he retired from the post of Circulation Manager for the news-sheet *The Collieston Blether*, but continued as Chief Reporter. This periodical, started in 1989, reports the doings of the Amenities Committee and of the Harbour Trustees and, as Jack Page, its editor and publisher, told me – 'anything newsworthy to do with the village'. It had two principal reporters – Rear Admiral Ritchie and John Robertson. Both have now retired.

The first *Collieston Blether* had, as its main story, details of how funds were being raised to 'Help Ensure the Pier is Always With Us'. That was the heading in July 1989. When the next edition appeared in February 1990 it was reported that the Pier Fund had raised more than the village's required share of the necessary £60,000. A donation of £10,000 from a resident, Mr Toby Sutton, had been a good boost to the amount earned through all sorts of money raising efforts ten-mile sponsored walks and dances among them.

Rear Admiral Ritchie has always played a considerable part. Having naval connections, he was able to organise two visits of naval survey ships at the time of gala days – always an important event for raising funds. The first gala day took place in 1958. People were allowed aboard the ships, and one of them took visitors to Peterhead where, after a buffet lunch organised by the ship's captain, they drove back to Collieston. Dances were organised during the ships' visits . These took place in the Collieston Hall which had originally been a Free Church.

Long ago Collieston

By 1994, the pier's centenary, extensive repairs were being made to the pier, and the contractor carrying out the work was asked to retrieve the casket placed beneath the foundation stone by Lady Gordon Cathcart, the time capsule of a hundred years ago. A sealed copper cylinder was recovered but, alas, the sea had penetrated the sealing and the contents, except for the coins, had been totally ruined. What vexation! A new time capsule was inserted with every possible precaution taken to ensure that in another hundred years there would not be a similar disappointment.

In the new steel capsule, which Rear Admiral Ritchie described as being like a shell, newspapers which that day were commemorating the 50th anniversary of D-Day, were inserted along with the newly burnished Victorian coins from the old capsule, and various contributions from the school and church.

The Collieston Amenities Committee as well as the Harbour Trustees have to keep on raising funds. To this end the Committee organise an annual gala and even provide implements such as grass cutting machines which volunteers use to keep the village and its surroundings clean and tidy. For the Pier Fund Rear Admiral Ritchie organises a biannual art exhibition in the Community Centre.

Throughout the years Collieston has had many social activities. In 1952, the writer of the third *Statistical Account* recorded the existence of a community club with a membership of 65, 31 of whom were under 18. Classes were held in leatherwork, woodwork, dressmaking, basketry, plastics and Scottish Country Dancing. The men had a Recreation Club which met in the Tea Room. They played card games, dominoes, darts and billiards. These organisations held whist drives, dances and concerts. Young men formed a football club.

As today, there was one general merchant's shop combined with a post office, but in 1952 Collieston had also a bakery shop with tea-room. Bakers', butchers' and grocers' vans called.

In 1952, the water supply was pumped from springs at a small bay called Port Thuddan, south of the village. The North of Scotland Hydro-Electric Board had promised to supply electricity in the next three years. Doctors came from Ellon and a district nurse from Cruden Bay.

From this *Statistical Account* it can be seen that the Collieston community was a lively one. This is still very much the case 50 years on. For the under fives there is a group approved by the Scottish Executive as a registered provider of pre-school activities. At the opposite end of the time scale there is an Over-50s Club. The village women have a walking group locally known as the 'Wifie Walkers'. There is a Youth Club, Swimming Club and, of course, the Boules Club. The primary children are taken by school bus to Slains' two-teacher school and secondary pupils are bussed to Ellon Academy. There is a once a week bus service to Ellon.

Not only does Collieston have an active community spirit, but it continues to be a beautiful and picturesque village – a place of gentle charm.

CHAPTER SIX

Boddam

The village of Boddam, about three miles south of Peterhead, also at one time had a castle of which only a very small ruin remains upstanding. According to Councillor Sam Coull's information given on Boddam and District Community Council's web pages, Boddam Castle was one of Scotland's oldest castles. It was built in the sixteenth century by the Keith family of Ludquharn. From what is left, there appears to have been a courtyard, measuring 31m by 28m, between the high cliffs.

There is now a board displaying a floor plan of the castle as well as the layout speculations of the late Ian R. D. Bryce, FSA Scot. Some other archaeological historians do not agree with his ideas but, as no archaeological examination has been carried out, it is interesting to use Bryce's experience-informed conjectures to try to visualise the castle as it once might have been.

We can imagine a Solar or drawing room for the laird, a hall (12m x 5m), a kitchen (9m x 7m) with a large, two-metre deep fireplace in one wall. Ian Bryce thought there had been a tower in which a bell might have hung for calling men in from their work in the fields, or even for rallying reinforcements should the need arise. He did not think that the tower was used for living in or as a place of defence. Some of the rooms he visualised as store rooms. He thought there would perhaps have been an oubliette over the gateway from which invaders could have been attacked.

There is also a board which sets out the family's history, along with an artist's impression of how the castle may have looked in its heyday.

The Keiths of Ludquharn, who owned Boddam Castle, had their arms recorded in 1678–79 by the second baronet, Alexander, whose motto was 'Remember thy End'.

The Keiths had become lairds of the Ludquharn lands by the marriage of Gilbert Keith, great grandson of Sir Edward Keith, 10th Great Marischal of Scotland. Gilbert's third son, Andrew, followed him as laird of Ludquharn, and from him those lands passed on to his son, John, who died with James IV on Flodden Field in 1513.

Charles II enobled John's great grandson and created the Barony of Ludquharn.

Councillor Coull tells us that Sir William Keith, born in 1669 in Boddam Castle, was one of the most famous of the castle's last residents. Sir William apparently started off rather well, becoming Surveyor General for the Southern District of the Americas from 1713. He rose to Lieutenant Governor of Pennsylvania. But, alas, he fell from his pinnacle, returned to Britain as 'a discarded public official', being greatly in debt, and died in 1749 'in the Old Baily, a liberty or parole section of the Fleet Street Prison'.

The line ended with Robert, 5th Baronet, who died in 1771. His two sons had died before him. Robert had had a military career, serving in the Prussian Army as Lieutenant Colonel under his cousin, Field Marshal James Keith. After rising to the rank of Major General, he served with the Danish army.

Boddam Castle was last inhabited about the beginning of the eighteenth century. An old servant, who had been 30 years with the last inhabitant, Lady Keith, is quoted as saying of their surely very amicable relationship – 'There was never sae muckle atween us a' that time, as the deil speed the leear'.

The writer of the 1794 *Statistical Account* thought the castle may at one time have been a fortress – indeed there was one of its several cannons beside the remaining walls of his day. In 1868, when the son of the proprietor was having a trench dug in front of the entrance to the castle, large hinges thought to be those of a drawbridge were found.

However, Boddam was not to be without the presence of an aristocratic family. Lord Aberdeen, who became Prime Minister in 1852, had built at the south end of the village in 1840 'a small house on

Boddam Harbour in the 1970s, before renovation

the extreme edge of the cliff and looking down on the tumbling waves of the North Sea.' This was the Earl's Marine Villa or Buchan Ness Lodge which in the 1970s became the Earl's Lodge Hotel. On its flag-staff had waved a flag to salute Queen Victoria as her yacht passed, taking her to Aberdeen on the way to Balmoral Castle. It was here too on what Lord Aberdeen called his 'quarter deck walk' that he enjoyed looking at 'as many as 300 boats from Peterhead and 48 from Boddam – a very beautiful sight as they all passed close under the house'. In 1984, however, a fire reduced the building to the shell we see today.

Seemingly, the women of the village also spent time watching the movements of the fishing fleet. Lord Aberdeen approved of this and had granite 'seaties' erected by the shore front for the women to sit on.

When I visited the village in the 1970s I was told that, when Lord Aberdeen was seen approaching, the women hurried out to sit on the 'seaties' for he was not pleased if they were not occupied.

Lord Aberdeen also gave the village a barometer. In 1845 he had a pier built in the more northerly of the two harbours that existed, at that time separated from each other by a beach of small, rounded stones. It was through his influence that Boddam became a registered port.

As elsewhere 'castle and cottage' were linked at times of celebration. One such occasion occurred in February, 1863, when Lady Mary Gordon, daughter of the Earl of Aberdeen, married the Master of Polwarth and the newly-weds chose to spend the first night of their honeymoon in Buchan Ness Lodge.

In and around Boddam flags were hung and the school bell pealed merrily at intervals throughout the day. A herring boat decorated with flags was mounted on wheels and drawn by horses through the village and up to the top of nearby Stirling Hill.

When darkness fell at 6pm the boat, surrounded by other combustible material, was set alight by an 86-year-old woman, Mrs Imlah, who had the distinction of being the oldest tenant on Lord Aberdeen's estate. Having set the bonfire going, Mrs Imlah sang the 'Boatie Rows' and the audience of about 200 cheered. The bonfire blazed for some time and could be seen from many miles away.

Then the villagers returned home to get their lanterns with which they lined both sides of the route the newly-weds' carriage was to take to Buchan Ness Lodge. Having given the couple a resounding cheer as they entered the Lodge, the villagers returned to Boddam where they held a ball at which they danced till 6am. Boddam people seem to have always enjoyed to the full their limited times of respite from the hard toil of fisherfolk.

The Rev. Mr William Donald wrote in the 1840 *Statistical Account* that Boddam had originated as a settlement of Dutch fishermen in the time of William of Orange who ruled in England 1689–1702.

In the first *Statistical Account* of 1794, the Rev. Dr Moir reported that at that time there were five boats which paid rent to the proprietor and 30 men were employed working them. A short time before, a sixth boat had been lost at sea and the four men of her crew were drowned. Two smaller boats were used by old men. 'Many of the young men of that town are now sailors.'

Another occupation in Boddam had been the production of salt. Some traces of salt pans were still to be seen, and a nearby headland, Sattie's Head, was thought to have been so named because it was in the proximity of the salt manufacture.

Dr Moir, when he wrote, was agitating for the erection of a lighthouse. He had suggested that one be built on the top of Stirling Hill, which the ships used as a land-mark in daylight. However, the sea-faring people had told him this would not be suitable because it would not be seen when mist was on the sea so far beneath it.

It was not till 1827 that the Northern Lighthouse Board was persuaded to build Buchan Ness Lighthouse. It was to be made from granite quarried from Stirling Hill. Before this shipwrecks were common occurrences. Between November 1816 and March 1819 as many as 20 ships were wrecked on the Buchan coast, including the sloop *Marchioness of Huntly* at Boddam itself in 1817. Two petitions were put before the Northern Lighthouse Board, one in 1819 and one in 1822 from 'merchants, shipowners, shipmasters and others interested in shipping'.

Robert Robinson, who sold the Commissioners of Northern Lights the island called the Yards of Boddam in 1825, was most careful to safeguard 'the liberty and privilege to the fishermen of my village of Boddam of drawing up their boats on the sea beach on either side of the narrow channel connecting the said isthmus [island] with the main land and of drying fish upon the Rocks of the said isthmus . . . '

There was no foghorn till 1904. One woman, Mrs I. Buchan, remembered when she, as a little girl, ran out in fog to the back of the lighthouse where she and her companions beat tin basins with spoons to warn boats off the rocks. Mrs Buchan claimed that the horn was first blown on 10 December 1904 to celebrate a wedding in her family. Someone else was of the opinion that those first blasts were in honour of a birth in his family.

Through the day at the lighthouse the three lightkeepers and 'occasional' keeper kept the station and its equipment ship-shape, and watched for fog. At sunset, they climbed the 146 stone steps plus nine of an iron ladder to light the paraffin lamp which transmitted a beam of 900,000 candlepower.

Every 45 minutes the man on watch wound up the clockwork machinery that brought a heavy metal weight to the top of a never-ending chain that dangled almost the entire length of the tower. Round rolled the gigantic lens, circling completely once every 20 seconds on its mercury bath, and beams of light – like spokes of a great cart-wheel – revolved in the dark sky round their hub of light, or so it looked from close-up; there was no brilliant flash as appeared when viewed from a distance.

For five years, from 1961–66, I lived in one of the little flat-roofed houses below those revolving beams. In 1954, just after a full moon when the tides were high and the wind blew strong from the south-east, two waves collided, forming a 'doubler', which crashed over the foghorn and intervening rocks, and burst through the lighthouse wall, flooding what became our house. At the same time, James Stephen, one of the occasional keepers, was swept helplessly along till he managed to grab hold of a ladder lashed to a wall. On subsequent nights when moon, sea and wind were similarly combined, I used to prowl uneasily round the house, peering through the darkened panes and straining my ears to judge the whereabouts of the sea.

Across a concrete courtyard stood a twin house for the other assistant lightkeeper. The principal keeper lived in a separate block outwith the courtyard containing the tower. Joined to his house were store-rooms, a work-shop and the engine room – opposite our bedroom window. When the fog rolled in we heard the snarl of the roused engines, the whooshing first gasp as air was blasted into the foghorn's 'lungs', and then a series of three moans escaping every 90 seconds from the great, red horn 45 yards away on the grey rocks. To my surprise, each time, within minutes, I ceased to be aware of the horn's blasts, and had to pause and listen consciously to check if it was still blowing. I think the steady background noise of the engines took away all the eerie, haunting quality of a foghorn moaning through mist at a distance. It was always a surprise to walk over the 50-yard bridge to find the village often squatting in bright sunshine while the island was shrouded for days.

So by the time the Rev. William Donald wrote the second *Statistical Account* in 1840, his predecessor's anxiety about obtaining a lighthouse had been satisfactorily allayed. The Rev. William Donald's suggestion for a required amenity for Boddam was the making of a proper harbour. He was sure that if Boddam had a harbour 'it might soon be expected to become a large trading place'. It was thought at that time that 'a most commodious little harbour' could be made for £1,500 to £1,800. In a footnote the writer added that 'an extensive harbour has been contracted for, and is in the course of being erected'.

The next time we hear of a harbour for Boddam was in 1878 when the present harbour was built by Mr William Aiton, then proprietor of the village. Mr Aiton, a sub-contractor engaged in the making of the Suez Canal, also set up in the village a combined smithy, engineering shop and net factory. The handlooms installed in the net factory were not a success as people were unwilling to work them. Instead, widows and old men wove herring nets by hand, earning two shillings and sixpence for every 28lbs of twine used. Tragedy struck Mr Aiton's family during the construction of the harbour. His son was blown up on the site. Understandably, Mr Aiton lost heart in the project and handed the harbour over to the ownership of the village.

Even without a harbour, the village year was described in fishing seasons by the Rev. William Donald in 1840. Through the winter till Candlemas, 12 boats with six men to a boat fished for cod. They might catch from 1,200 to 1,800 fish, each fish being worth from fourpence to sixpence. From March to July, 22 small yawls, each crewed by four men and a boy, caught haddocks. A fair catch would be 25,000–30,000, according to the Rev. W. Donald; 2,500–3,000, according to Anson, which would earn £3–£4 per thousand. From July to September, 23 herring boats pursued the silver shoals, and made about £100 per boat per year.

Mr Donald says also that Boddam haddocks obtained 'a decided preference in the market, partly from the great care taken upon them by the people themselves, but in great measure owing to the rocks along the shore on which the fish are dried and which are quite clean and free from sand'. The preparation of the haddocks was indeed intricate – after being split, washed and salted, they were spread in heaps on the beach. Then, they were carried to the rocks and spread out one by one. Every night, and if it rained during the day, they were gathered together and taken in. When dry enough, they were prepared for sale by being smoked on spits over peat fires, put into a pile and pressed down.

Before a market had been found for the summer haddocks, the fishermen had had to go 'deep sea fishing' at a bank a long way off the coast, and try to catch ling, cod, turbot, skate and other flat fish. Dog fish were procured for their livers which provided oil.

By about 1880, when the height of prosperity was reached, there were 151 boats and 476 fishermen.

There was a noticeboard on which fishermen had to notify their intentions to launch or haul the 52ft herring boats or the yawls for the white fishing in the winter. When a launching or hauling was announced then every man with a share in a boat, or in a boat's nets, had to turn out to help – illness being the only accepted excuse. A fine was imposed on any defaulter.

Peter Anson in his book, *Fishing Boats and Fisher Folk on the East Coast of Scotland*, published in 1930, remarks that – 'not so very long ago there were as many as 85 large herring drifters here and 13 curing yards'.

In 1970, Mr and Mrs John Noble Stephen of Boddam could remember five boatbuilding yards and 11 curing yards. Mrs Stephen showed me her small, sharp, wooden-handled gutting knife, and told me of the life of a fishergirl in the herring industry. At the first sight of the boats returning from sea she would dress in her oilskin, pleated skirt with breast-high bib, knee-length leather boots and headsquare.

If a 'gutter', she bandaged fully the thumb and two forefingers of each hand with yellow calico tied with cotton. 'Packers' rolled up every finger over the tips and half-way down. Two 'gutters' and a 'packer' made up a crew. They took up their positions behind five tubs in the curing yard. In Boddam a flag was hoisted to tell nearby farmers when to come with their carts and transport the fish from the shore to the 11 curing yards. Mr Patrick Sellar's grandfather, an extraordinarily versatile man – fisherman, curing yard owner, pilot, harbourmaster and boatbuilder – had his own private communication link. He took with him two carrier pigeons. One brought word of where he had shot his nets, and the other flew back with the amount of his catch.

On arrival at the yard the herring were emptied into oblong boxes called 'farlans'. As they poured into the 'farlans', a cooper sprinkled them with salt. Then they were gutted with small, sharp, wooden-handled knives, sometimes as quickly as 58 per minute, and tossed into one of the five tubs according to size.

Early in the season there would be a quantity of 'dead small'. Next to these, in ascending order of size, came the 'matties' (at 9 1/2 inches long), 'mattie full', 'full' and 'large full'. Towards the close of the season there would be a further selection called 'spent' (or spawned) herring.

The crew carried their tubs to the appropriate large 'roosin' tub into which the packer poured scoopfuls of salt as the sorted fish were emptied in. She then mixed and tumbled them thoroughly in the salt. Next, they were firmly packed, layer about with salt, in the barrels. Mrs Stephen demonstrated with matchsticks the pattern for packing them.

At the end of that day, probably past midnight, the girls would lay the covers, or 'heads', on their barrels by the light of oil lamps. The following morning started, sometimes as early as 6am, by topping up the barrels, for the fish had settled overnight.

The coopers would then 'put on the heads', and the barrels were left for ten days. After this came the final filling up. The coopers bored a hole about a quarter of the way up the sides of the barrels, and through this the salt pickle was drained off. The 'heads' were again removed, the barrels filled to the top with more fish and salt, 'heads' fastened down, the salt pickle poured back through the hole and a bung pushed into position.

The girls earned threepence an hour for this lengthy process, carried on out-of-doors with no shelter, and for them that was not yet the end of those barrels. One day a brazier would be lit in the yard, and the crews waited on tenterhooks for what was, one might say, their term examination. This yard owner would inform the local fishery officer that he had a 'parcel of herring' ready for branding.

This official would then arrive with his branding irons. He chose a barrel here and there for inspection, and had some opened at the top,

Fishergirls working at the herring

some at the bottom. Then, from each barrel the officer would pick a herring and take a bite out of its back. By its firmness, the brightness of its silver scales and its taste to his experienced palate, he decided if the Crown Brand would be granted.

This brand mark signified that the fishery officer guaranteed that the herring would keep in any climate for 12 months. It was only applicable to Scottish fisheries and continued in use till 1950. Schooners such as the *Industry*, owned by Mr Patrick Sellar's grandfather, would then cross to the Baltic countries full of branded herrings and return laden with oak to build more boats.

Coopers in more prosperous times for the North East fishing industry

The tasting part alone would, perhaps, discourage most of us from becoming a fishery officer, but the officer in Peterhead told me that, from 1808, when the brand was constituted, competition for the limited number of posts was fierce. It was the top of the tree for men already qualified as coopers. They were not even deterred by the fact that in the early days, in some places, fishery officers had to go about their business armed with blue-painted police-type batons for protection.

It would seem that there were times – in an earlier period – when the fishermen of Boddam too had to face violence. Mr Patrick Sellar's grandmother ground her mustard seed with the cannonball of a French press-gang ship that had chased some boats from Boddam.

However, by 1900 all that bustling, industrious way of life had ceased. In a series of newspaper reports in 1928 on the decay of the fishing industry in the North East fishing villages, the correspondent states – 'Nowhere, however, is the decline more pronounced or the distress more acute than at Boddam.' There were now only a dozen boats, most of which had motor engines. No curing was done at all. An old inshore fisherman told the writer – 'The trawlers have absolutely spoiled us.' He showed him the catch of three men on a motorboat after two and a half hours' fishing – one small codling! A day's average catch was one or two boxes of codlings, bringing in about 30/- out of which they had to meet their expenses.

When Peter Anson wrote in 1929, he said that he had found Boddam 'silent and deserted, with grass growing on the piers of its harbour built half a century ago or more to accommodate the fleet of boats which filled it.' At the time of his visit, 15 line boats still went to the small line fishing, and the old men 'who seem to belong to another age' caught lobsters and crabs for a living. When he spoke to the old men about the decline of the fishing, they blamed the advent of the trawler. He, however, thought that perhaps a more probable explanation was the proximity to Peterhead where 'all fishing has been concentrated and whither many of the younger and more energetic fishermen have migrated'.

The net factory continued to exist. About one hundred years ago it was taken over by the Sellar family who concentrated on salmon fishing. Until the 1970s a fourth generation built salmon cobbles there and fixed nylon nets to their ropes. Six men were employed all the year round, and 12 more when they went out from Macduff to catch salmon. The factory premises were up for sale in the 1970s, and the family moved permanently to Macduff.

As noted, the Boddam villagers did not miss the opportunity of a celebration when Lord Aberdeen's daughter married. The same was the case when any of their own number married. Miss Kathleen Macleod, daughter of an ex-minister in Boddam, and resident in the village in the 1960s, fortunately interviewed elderly Boddam people who could remember wedding celebrations in the late nineteenth century. She recorded her findings and they eventually appeared in the

Transactions of The Buchan Field Club, the chairman of which society gave me permission to draw upon them.

Seemingly, courtship in Boddam was carried on as secretly as possible, and the intention to marry only announced when the marriage banns were to be proclaimed in the 'Muckle Kirk', as the established church in Peterhead is called. After the calling or 'the crying' of the banns had been arranged or 'booked', there started a series of celebrations. That evening the 'Buiken Pairty' was held in the home of the bride-to-be. Close friends and relatives were invited for tea, talk and parlour games.

The next day the young couple, accompanied by their parents, either walked to Peterhead or in later times took a bus drawn by three horses. Miss Macleod had been told that at an earlier period the families did this journey by boat, but after disaster struck two boats on such a trip the sea journey was no longer used.

The purpose of this outing was to buy furnishings for the new household-to-be and clothes for the wedding. The groom and the fathers were expected to buy the furniture, and it was the groom's duty to provide coloured dress material for the bride and her two bridesmaids – who were known in Boddam as 'the maidens' – as well as for his mother and mother-in-law-to-be, though those two matrons would not be present at the wedding ceremony. The bride bought white shirts for the groom and two best men – the 'gweedmen'.

During the next week or two the bride and one maiden, and the groom and a gweedman went around the village inviting people to the wedding. This was called the 'biddin' of the guests, and because families were so large at that time only the two older members were invited.

The next celebrated event was the 'Decoratin' o' the Hoose' which was held on the eve of the wedding. Before this the heavier pieces of furniture had been already placed inside, and now an aunt of the bride and an aunt of the groom waited in the nearly empty house to receive helpers who carried in the other items of furnishing. This involved a kind of ritual. The bridegroom was expected first, bringing a bolster, and was followed by the gweedmen each carrying a pillow. As the groom made his entrance one of the aunts broke a plate or a bowl for

The 'shippies' being sailed on the Den Dam above Boddam

luck. The bride, not being allowed to see her home till after the wedding ceremony, tried, as did the groom after bringing his bolster, to go into hiding to escape the 'feet washin' – a custom dreaded by many.

Meanwhile, the helpers set the house to rights, hanging religious pictures and Bible texts, and arranging ornaments – perhaps china dogs or china figurines of popular figures such as Robert Burns, a ship in a bottle and most likely an amber-handled, round kettle of burnished brass. In long gone days, the floors were of well trodden down earth sprinkled with sand. Later, there would be a wooden floor with an old sail which had been painted and decorated laid over it.

Of course, some interested party made a concoction of tar, blacklead, feathers and treacle or syrup in a tub, and if the bride and groom were found they were forced to have their feet immersed in this messy mixture. This usually took place in the bride's home and caused great hilarity to all bystanders.

At last the wedding day dawned and the gweedmen hung flags and bunting across the street from the bride's home. Each of the young couples' homes then hosted a 'breakfast' of boiled salt fish and oatcakes. The guests were the aunts and uncles.

Later in the forenoon the married women relatives made up the beds in the new house and with other married friends prepared the long tables in the village hall for the wedding feast. In very early times two feasts were held – one at 4pm when the couple and their guests arrived from the church, and a late feast at 8pm. By the end of the nineteenth century marriages were being held entirely in the hall, and there was only one meal in the evening. Miss Macleod thought that the reason for this was the fact that more Boddam men were then learning trades and the evening would have suited the guests so employed to attend. When the majority had been fishermen, weddings were planned to take place when there were lulls in the fishing year. In 1840, Boddam people had the reputation of marrying between the ages of 18 and 20, producing large families and living to a good old age.

When it was time for the bride to set out for church or hall either the school or church bell rang out. A procession was formed of people in pairs behind the bride who had a gweedman on each arm. The bride and her attendants proceeded to the end of the hall or to the choir space in the church. If the ceremony was to take place in the hall, the bride's friends took seats at the already set tables. Shortly after the first procession was seated, the groom, with a maiden on each arm, led his procession of friends and relatives who took seats prepared for them.

Silence obtained, the bridal party lined up in front of the minister who performed the ceremony with no musical accompaniment. Miss Macleod commented that the absence of music was strange, for fisherfolk love to sing.

One of Miss Macleod's interviewees was in her 80s, but she remembered seeing her mother break a piece of fruit cake shielded by a handkerchief on the forehead of a niece – a ritual carried out to ensure the bride would always have 'plenty'.

Then the company enjoyed the feast of thick slices of bread, lumps of cheese, butter and jam and several kinds of fancy cakes. There was no actual wedding cake, but as fruit cake became more common it was served. Miss Macleod could recall a wedding she attended where there was a cake of thick shortbread iced with white icing on which was pictured a herring boat with sails, a sample of the kind of vessel used up to about 1910.

When there was an early and later meal, the guests at the first sitting left the hall when finished, except for the married women who washed up dishes, tidied and prepared the tables for the feast at 8pm. Between the feasts the guests visited the newly-weds in their new home and drank toasts to them in wine. When the later feast was over, the floor was cleared for games or dancing. The games were mostly played in rings with the choosing of partners.

After all the hilarity, some of the young people went to the new house where they helped the newly-weds into bed amidst much jollity. This ceremony, 'the Beddin', ended with the bride throwing one of her stockings from the bed. Whoever caught it was supposed to be next to marry.

There was no honeymoon, but the two maidens stayed with the couple for a few days after the wedding helping with housework.

The night following the wedding, special friends were invited by the gweedmen and maidens to come for yet another celebration. This was the 'tatties and herrin'. Salt herring were boiled on top of potatoes in their jackets and eaten with tea to drink and fancy cakes to follow.

The last of the series of wedding rituals was 'the kirkin', on the Sunday following the wedding, when the newly-weds were escorted to church by the gweedmen. The maidens were left at home to cook the dinner. The following morning the maidens departed to their own homes and the young couple settled down to a life of hard toil.

Another time of celebration was 'Aul' Eel' – Old Yule. On 7 January, 1890, *The Sentinel and Buchan Journal* reported 'Auld Yule Festivities at Boddam. The Fishermen's Soiree.' On 12 January, 1866, the event on Old Christmas Day was described as the 'Temperance Soiree'. With the passing of the years, there had surely been radical changes. According to Miss Macleod, the date of celebration was 5 January which had been Christmas Day before the eighteenth century change in the calendar. Indeed, the local paper reported on 7 January, 1899, that 'Thursday the 5th was celebrated in the usual custom, and the whole village was on holiday.' It goes on to tell how in the forenoon the small 'shippies' were sailed in the Den Dam. The 'shippies' were model boats built in true boat-building fashion by the men of the village. The men raced them on behalf of sons or young male relatives. In the 1960s every boy received a prize at the 'Boatie Social' held in the New Year.

Miss Macleod described the prizes of the past – very utilitarian ones such as shirts, stockings and scarves – handed out at the Dam. In her time, they were presented at the 'Boatie Social' in the Public Hall, and consisted of items such as pencil cases and torches. In the 1960s the boys were given toys. I myself remember one little boy getting a plastic Noddy House.

But by the 1960s the 'Sailin' o' the Shippies' was taking place on a suitable day in summer. The days of having to cut up the ice on the Den Dam with wires before the boats could sail were over. Though winter cold had not deterred Boddam fisherfolk from making the most of the event. According to Miss Macleod some 'hardy onlookers' had boiled their kettles and picnicked on the braes beside the Dam.

The 1899 newspaper report went on to describe the rest of Auld Yule Day. In the afternoon the village flute band was transported through the village streets and up Stirling Hill seated on a boat erected on a lorry pulled by a beautifully decorated horse. Their arrival was the signal to everybody at the Den Dam to make their way to a certain park and take part in games of barrow-wheeling, climbing the greasy pole and others, and so pass the afternoon.

Mr Alfred Buchan, one of the occasional lightkeepers at Buchan Ness Lighthouse, told me in the 1960s that in his day the flute band marched in the morning to the Den Dam behind a horse-drawn lorry carrying the 'boaties', and followed by a procession. At the head of the procession was the fishermen's committee and, after them, came everybody else. A barrel of apples was taken along for distribution at the scene. This was the Boddam custom each New Year's Day in Alfie's youth, whatever the weather.

When evening came, the villagers went to the Public Hall. There a chairman, sometimes a professional man from Peterhead, but in this report, a fisherman, reviewed the state of the fishing industry, the farming and the granite industries of Boddam and its close environment over the past year. His remarks were followed by a concert. A similar report in 1860 gave details of the entertainment. There were songs by a choir and by solo singers, who sang pieces such as 'Annie Laurie', 'Rothesay Bay', and 'The Weary Pund o' Towe'. Speeches entitled 'Good Cheer' and 'The Day's Sport'; dramatic sketches like 'Old Fat Jose' and 'John M'Rae's Displeasure in Married Life' and a humorous reading of 'Five Feet Nine' amused the audience.

After the concert came the dance which was 'kept up with much spirit till far into the morning'. No meal is reported in the newspaper, but in Miss Macleod's article, 'Aul' Christmas Customs', the festive evening was called the Ran Dan, and there was tea and fancy cakes – the tea being poured out of the ubiquitous, round brass kettles with amber handles. 'The dances danced,' wrote Miss Macleod, 'were polkas, reels, petronella, strip-the-willow, Flooers o' Edinburgh, lancers, quadrilles, the schottische, and later, the waltz.'

Miss Macleod could find only one food preparation that was made for Yule-tide. This was called 'Christmas breid' and consisted of specially dressed oatcakes. Dry oatmeal, caraway seeds and hot fat mixed with milk were spread over the oatcakes. The cake was then cooked on the lower side on a girdle. The upper side was cooked by being toasted in front of the fire.

Speaking to an octogenarian in 1957, Miss Macleod discovered the 'kyarlin' custom. This happened on 4 January. The effigy of an old woman was set up on the chimney of the man who'd had the smallest catch of fish that day. Miss Macleod said that this custom was on its way out 70 years ago – that would have been about 1887.

On the evening of the 4th, the flute band marched through the village playing Scottish tunes and all sorts of mischievous pranks were played by youths. Boats were hauled from the beach up into the village and occasionally a live cockerel would be put down somebody's chimney.

Santa Claus came to Boddam from the 1870s, but not on 4 January – only on Hogmanay. The only present-giving Miss Macleod heard about were pinafores and aprons given to girls and women. Any girl or woman not receiving this gift was called an 'eel jade'.

However, for about 65 to 75 years, that is from the 1880s, Miss Macleod said that Christmas services were held in churches, children's socials took place in the village and Christmas trees appeared. Then, Boddam School, falling in line with other schools, no longer had 5 January as a holiday.

There was a school in Boddam from at least 1794 when there was a teacher instructing about 20 children to read English. In 1840 there were few young men who could not 'read, write and cast up accounts in a very creditable way'. In 1876, the predecessor of the present school was rebuilt and had an average attendance of 169. At one period, one of its five teachers had to distinguish her Bobby Stephens by number. There were 13 of them! Because there were so many people with the same surname middle names were often used instead of surnames and distinguishing tee names, or nicknames, were prevalent. John Noble Stephen was known as Johnny Noble. There was one family of Stephens known as the Piths, Jimmy Pith, Alec Pith, and a family of Cordiners all referred to as Don – Peter Don, Isy Don and so on. Before my time in Boddam in the 1960s there had been 'Bell's Peter', 'Grocer's Jimmy' and 'Jinty's Jock'.

New surnames would have been added to the school roll in plenty when an RAF camp was built on the village's western edge in 1953. In 1975, out of 189 pupils, 64 were from 'the camp'. RAF Buchan also provided some employment but now the camp is about to be closed.

When we visited the village in the 1970s it was to find the harbour drained dry. It was not usual to find a village by the sea with neither boats nor harbour, but in 1975 such was the case in Boddam, only four miles south of the busy port of Peterhead. The dusty brown crater that used to be the harbour was flanked on either side by stout red noticeboards on which in neat, white letters was printed the warning – DANGER – BLASTING – WATCH FOR THE FLAGMAN.

On a quiet Sunday afternoon, round the perimeter, like monsters in wait, lurked massive, earth-moving vehicles, while down in the crater, one of their number buzzed and snickered and roared as if it had toppled into the abyss and was frantically but ineffectually trying to get out. A great, cumbersome brown barricade of metal stakes sealed the harbour mouth. Bewildered herring gulls wheeled and swooped low as though peering into the desolation where once they bathed and floated and fished.

All this had resulted from the arrival of a fairy godmother for the village in the guise of the North of Scotland Hydro Electricity Board, for, contrary to appearance, these and other cataclysmic events were to leave Boddam in a greatly improved condition.

Now Boddam has a very fine harbour and, as far as I can see, the Hydro Board have done all they promised when they set about building their huge power station, costing millions of pounds, which now stands to the north of the village. To cool the engines, water is pumped from the harbour and the Hydro Board paid handsomely and eternally for this privilege. They scooped out a channel in the harbour, so giving the village deep water berthing facilities, and built a slip-way to facilitate the launching and hauling of boats. Ground was levelled for the boats to rest on, the storm-damaged pier was mended and, with the cleared up rubble, they formed a grassy plateau along the street that edges the cliff-top.

I think, however, that it should have been called the 'Boddam Power Station' rather than the 'Peterhead Power Station'.

Sandford Lodge, the Georgian mansion of the Boddam estate, was preserved and, while work at the Power Station was going on, housed single engineers working there. The Lodge was originally the home of James Skelton, Sheriff substitute of Peterhead, whose son, Sir John Skelton wrote several books, including *The Crooked Meg*, a story of smuggling in the North East.

While there was no harbour, the boats – two belonging to full-time fishermen and about 20 to part-time and pleasure boat-men – were stored and their owners were compensated for the inconvenience.

When I lived at Buchan Ness Lighthouse, the little streets and fascinating labyrinths off them were usually quiet and empty. Many a time the only people I saw, and they always had a friendly greeting, were the old men who sat on the granite 'seaties' looking out to sea. Boddam streets were at one time, with the exception of Harbour Street, lettered – A street, B street and so on. It was only when the County Council took over that they were named.

The shops were cottages serving as such. There were 'Sophia's' and 'Janet's' for knitting wool, clothing and presents from Boddam – usually depicting the lighthouse. Sophia and Janet were not only the proprietors, managerial and sales staff, but they made you feel they were glad to have a visit from you. It was the same when you went to Mrs Sutherland's for groceries or the post office for stamps or a cake baked by the postmaster's father. There was a butcher, a baker and a second grocer. A sea-food factory conveniently situated by the harbour and the net factory were the only industries.

Cricket was traditionally the Boddam game. The Boddam Victoria Cricket Club had been formed about 1860, and had risen to Grade 1 in the Aberdeenshire League. Fishermen of Boddam, and quarriers and polishers from Stirling Village would often set off on their Saturday half-day on the two-hour journey by horse brake to Fraserburgh, play cricket, and return in the small hours of Sunday morning. When Mr Stephen of Stirling Village told me about this in 1970, he said that whereas there were 20 players in his day there were now only 16 and they were in Grade 3.

Other traditional leisure activities still enjoyed were 'tatties and herrin' and 'the boaties' sometimes called 'the shippies'.

Today, there is a post office, two general merchants and the garage has expanded from being merely a repair workshop, as it was in the 1960s, to being a place where cars can be bought and sold, and where it's also possible to buy such modern equipment as stereos and the like. There are two hotels in the village: the Seaview and the Buchan Ness Hotel where young people in the 1950s gathered from many directions to dance to the music of 'The Ambassadors' or 'Charlie Fyfe and his Band' in what was known as the Boddam Ballroom, which opened in 1953. Before that dances were held in the Village Hall. The dances in fashion in the Boddam Ballroom were – the Eightsome Reel, Strip the Willow, the Old Fashioned Waltz and, coming into vogue, were the Modern Waltz, the Quickstep and jiving.

A library, now boasting a very fine chiming clock added amidst considerable controversy, was built in 1991–92. More seats have appeared in various parts of the village. New railings have been erected round the base of the War Memorial. Sheltered housing has been built. In March 2002 it was decided to refurbish a play area and erect a Gateway at the south entrance to the village as part of the commemorations of the Queen's Golden Jubilee. Football and cricket are played. According to a list in the library there is a Boddam Karate Club, a playgroup, Youth Club and Senior Citizens Club. Not mentioned is a pack of Wolf Cubs attended by some children from Cruden Bay.

But, in the harbour where there was in the nineteenth century quite a sizeable fishing fleet, there are only four boats that fish full-time for crabs and lobsters. A fisherman told me there is very little white fish for inshore fishing boats to catch. He blamed the great number of seals for the shortage in supply. About 20 or so part-time boats also use Boddam's very fine harbour which I recently found to have been greatly extended and improved since the 1960s when I used to push a pram round it.

The small sea-food factory of that time is now a much larger, more impressive looking place.

The lighthouse, like all Scottish lighthouses, is now automatic. The foghorn of my time has been blasted from the rocks, and a modern electronic one, which I always thought sounded very inferior to the old one, has been silenced.

As with all six Buchan villages revisited, Boddam's heyday as a fishing port, for which no doubt it came into being originally, is long over.

Present-day Buchan Ness Lighthouse, Boddam,
with Peterhead Power Station in the background

CHAPTER SEVEN

Work in the Villages' Hinterland

As the women from the fishing villages (who, according to Thomas Pennant in 1769, often had neither shoes nor stockings, but wore many rings on their fingers) walked into the countryside to sell or barter their fish for eggs, oatmeal and dairy products, they saw a very different rural hinterland from that which we, in the twenty-first century, see.

Very little of the land in the eighteenth and nineteenth centuries was enclosed and, where it was, there were no fences or stone walls, but dykes of earthen sods. Where cultivated, it lay in ridges and furrows. Small, underfed, pot-bellied horses were tethered with fir tethers made of splints of fir cut from logs found in bogs and twisted together, or ropes made from hairs from the tails of cattle. The fir tethers had another use when finished as tethers – they then became fir candles.

The fisherwomen would have seen men out ploughing with heavy, unwieldy wooden ploughs pulled by 10 to 12 oxen. It was not till about 1790 that lighter, better fashioned implements of iron were made and the wooden teeth of the harrows began to be made of iron. Then the number of oxen could be decreased, first of all with one pair of horses replacing those next to the plough, later by two pairs of horses and so on. However, in 1792, and indeed in exceptional cases, as late as the beginning of the nineteenth century, ploughs could still be seen pulled by 12 oxen.

Horses had always pulled the lighter harrows, and carried a creel on each side to cope with the draught work on the farm. Wheeled conveyances were very rare and of little use since there were no roads. Well into the eighteenth century the wooden teeth of the harrows began to be made of iron. Incidentally, lack of roads made the transport of heavy goods, like coal, for example, almost impossible to places inland. Coastal places had no such difficulty, for supplies of all kinds, no matter how heavy or bulky, could be transported by sea. Country people were therefore dependent on peats and wood for their fires.

After the 1745 Jacobite Rebellion road-building started. Subduing armies had to have roads to march along. Wheeled carts came into use, but horses could still be seen with creels hanging on either side or sacks of grain slung over their backs as they returned from the mill.

For the village of New Deer, one carrier with a horse and creels went once a week to load up with provisions in Aberdeen. Sometimes the carrier did not even have a horse, but carried a creel on his own back. In 1793, the minister reported that now three or four carriers, each with a cart and two horses, were being employed.

The fisherwomen from the coastal villages would have called at the doors of the small cottages consisting of two rooms – a but and ben. Sometimes these dwellings were made of turf and bits of wood, cemented together with mud (or clay mixed with straw), with roofs made of turf and heather, held in place with straw ropes, but some, as noted by Pennant in 1769, were built with bricks of clay and straw and roofed with wooden planks with slates fixed on top. Invited inside, the fisherwoman would warm herself at a central, open peat fire and perhaps see the few cooking utensils by the dim light of dried and peeled fir candles.

There would be very little money, if any, to buy fish or anything else. In 1791, in the parish of Slains a farm labourer earned tenpence a day without food, or sixpence with it. Masons were slightly better off, earning one shilling and sixpence a day without food being provided. Tailors earned fivepence a day with food.

No doubt, on their travels those early fisherwomen met many others trudging through the countryside endeavouring to make a living. There were chapmen with their large packs containing all sorts of household and personal items otherwise unobtainable to the countryfolk. Sometimes amongst the various contents would be chap books, costing a penny or halfpenny each and telling stories and ballads such as 'The Wise Men of Gotham' and 'Witty Exploits of Mr

George Buchanan, the King of Scots Fool'. Then there were tinkers who made tin utensils and horners who made spoons out of horns. Tailors too travelled about from house to house obtaining woollen cloth and making clothes out of it. Those craftsmen could also be encountered at the fairs.

Near the cottages there were usually small yards in which the people grew green and red kail, herbs, flowers and plants such as honeysuckle, southernwood, peppermint, wormwood and docks. In a book entitled *The Secret Lore of Plants and Flowers* I found that honeysuckle was believed to have great healing power and could charm away boils. Southernwood was included in an old recipe for a hair tonic. Wormwood was in a list of plants used in making perfumed oils and could be combined with camomile to make a concoction to cure stomach upsets. An old rural superstition believed that poisonous plants and their antidotes always grew in close proximity. This was thought to be the case with nettles and dock, the latter being able to ameliorate the nettle's sting. Dock leaves too were applied to grazes and bruises and for this reason were grown in the yards. In the ploughed rigs the fisherwomen would have seen crops of barley, bere,

A fisherwoman with her creel

oats, pease and turnips with some wheat and potatoes. About the beginning of the nineteenth century, scythes had replaced sickles and instead of taking four and a half to five days to harvest one acre of wheat with a sickle, a man with a scythe could do as much in two to two and a half days.

Hardworking farmers gathered stones from their land and built them into dykes to enclose fields. Bricks and tiles came to be made and instead of draining the land by making it into rigs, they drained more successfully with tile drains, and levelled their fields.

As the nineteenth century went on, the fisherwomen would have seen pairs of horses pulling iron ploughs, sowing machines and reaping machines. They would have seen fields of turnips and swedes to feed the improved breeds of cattle.

There would still be the roughly constructed but and bens, but also farmhouses built of stone with slated roofs, proper chimneys and, inside, proper floors.

While going on to more profitable farming methods the lairds got rid of smaller, poorer places, and encouraged their sub-tenants to gather into little communities from which they could provide their richer neighbours with general and seasonal labour on their bigger farms. Craft workers also gathered there – blacksmiths, millers, millwrights, butchers, bakers, saddlers, tailors and shopkeepers.

By and by villages grew or were planned by the landowners to specialise in crafts such as linen and woollen manufacture.

The position of villages were firstly determined by the presence of a good water supply and then by the positioning of roads that made transport easier or indeed possible. Rivers and canals too were places by which people settled, for again the waterways made transport of necessities easier. As the century progressed, bigger and more important changes occurred. Steam ships were joined by steam trains, and on their routes and at their termini, some villages became towns while those not touched by railway lines tended to stagnate.

The railways appeared to be entirely to the advantage of the rural communities, but there was another side to the story. Now the smaller places and their craftsmen found themselves competing with the products and services of bigger centres. Some competed successfully.

Others did not, and people had often either to move to bigger, more prosperous places where work was available or emigrate.

As for the fisherwomen, with the advent of the railways, they could either ride with their creels in relative ease, or simply let the trains carry their fish to more distant markets.

The twentieth century started with Scotland's farming in a state of economic depression. Bad harvests succeeded each other, and steamships and railways brought grain from America and frozen beef and mutton from Australasia which could be sold at lower prices than the home-grown products. From the 1880s even top-quality cattle from the north-east could earn less than previously. The Great War brought an economic boom but, as happened with the fishing industry, this had petered out by 1921.

Like the fishing industry too, the farming industry at the beginning of the century was feeling the effects of technological advance on its economic life. Sickles, scythes and flails were being replaced by reapers, binders and steam mills; horses by tractors.

In farming, the year was dominated by the seasons. Mr Stephen, a farmer whom I interviewed quite recently, gave a succinct review of a year on his farm.

We did the ploughing, that was usually in November, December, January. Spring starts about the middle of March and April with sowing the seeds of barley and oats. Summer – we cut the hay about the end of June into coles then into rucks. When hay's finished we start the harvest, usually in September. Then winter – taking the cattle inside for the winter and ploughing again. There's been a lot of changes in the last 50 years. Back in the 30s it was slavery for the people. When my father was working on a farm in Rothienorman in 1933 his wage was one pound a week and there were nine of us – nine of a family.

There was a hierarchy among farm-workers. The horseman, for example, was in a superior position to the bailie, who looked after the cattle, and right at the foot of the ladder was the orraman who did all the jobs not apportioned to those above him. Mr Stephen told of how entry into the farmhouse kitchen for meals was always made in order of rank. First would come the foreman, next the horseman, then the bailie and last the orraman. The kettle of boiling water was passed round also according to rank, for each man to make his brose.

I spoke to Mr Burnett, a retired farm-servant who'd worked 33 years for a farmer who owned a number of farms. He told me that, when he started in the 1950s, the staff consisted of 13 workers – 'three horsemen, four cattlemen, two tractor men, four orramen'. Later in the interview Mr Burnett revealed that there had also been a grieve and under grieve. He seemed not to include them in his tally of workers. Possibly they were seen as administrators as distinct from workers. It was they who set the workers to their various tasks each morning. The farm owner never appeared. 'The grieve lived in the farmhouse,' commented Mr Burnett. Perhaps this arrangement placed the grieve in a slightly higher echelon of society in the eyes of the others.

On most farms there was a kitchie deem who, besides doing work in the farmhouse, had to do some outdoor work as well. Like the fisherwomen, the farming women worked hard – from the actual

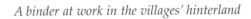

A binder at work in the villages' hinterland

hand-milking of the cows, to making the butter and cheese, and baking scones and oatcakes to eat with the dairy products. The fisherwomen were essential to their men's livelihood. Likewise, the farming women's earnings were an indispensable part of the family income.

Mrs McRobbie, a 90 year old, and Mrs Forman, an 88 year old, told of their lives as kitchie deems in the 1920s. They said they had been addressed by their surnames and were regarded as inferiors by upstairs maids and their employers. Again, the presence of a hierarchical system appears in the farming community.

The day of Mrs McRobbie and Mrs Forman had started at 5am when they had to begin their duties by cleaning out and lighting the fire, milking the cows and preparing brose for the single farm-workers who lived in the 'chaumer', a room in the steading. Besides preparing the meals for the entire household, the kitchie deem had to scrub the kitchen's stone floor, make up beds, wash and iron clothes, and do all the work involved in keeping chaumer and farmhouse clean and in order. Mrs McRobbie also remembered setting up peats to dry at the peat banks, stooking sheaves in the harvest field and forking sheaves at the building of the stacks, called 'rucks' in Aberdeenshire.

Two instances of class distinction in action were still poignantly remembered. Mrs McRobbie had ambitions to play the fiddle. She set about teaching herself, but was firmly told she had not been employed to do that. The other instance recalled was when she bought fish from the fish van and cooked it for the household. All the fish had to go upstairs. She was not allowed any.

Mrs Forman had initially helped her mother who was also a kitchie deem. Sometimes Mrs Forman had to go from farm to farm to gather potatoes and, surprising for the 1920s, she also clipped sheep for which job she always wore bib and brace dungarees; she was the first woman in the area to do so.

Neither of my kitchie deem interviewees mentioned helping with the hoeing of turnips which took place about the middle of June till the middle of July. The workers hoed together in long lines each with a long-handled hoe, pushing out some plants to give the remainder space to grow and swell ready to feed the cattle, when, about the end of October, they would be brought in from the fields to winter in the byre. Then the horses and carts brought the turnips into the turnip-shed. Some turnips had to be sliced by a hand-operated implement called 'a neep hasher' for cows that had difficulty in chewing, or for calves. Mr Stephen showed me one of those implements and explained that a hasher that cut turnips into even smaller sizes was used when preparing them to feed sheep.

Hay was the first crop to be harvested. This, in Aberdeenshire, took place usually in July, but could be held up by bad weather till August. Odd jobs were usually done in August such as the painting of steading doors and windows, and cutting rushes to thatch stacks.

By the end of August, weather being suitable, preparations started to harvest the corn. 'Roads' were cut around the edges of the cornfields with scythes. Before the horse-drawn reaper came into use, the horsemen would scythe the crop, which was then gathered into sheaves by women coming behind them. The women made bands of corn to tie each sheaf together, but only laid each sheaf on its band, leaving the tying to the men who built the sheaves into stooks. The same procedure was followed when the horse-drawn reapers appeared, but the arrival of the binder did away with all need of people to gather into sheaves, make bands or tie up the sheaves. Binders were on the scene in the 1920s.

When the stooks were dry and ready, the horses and carts again came into use, and carried home the harvest to the stack-yard where the skilled job of building waterproof stacks took place. With luck, the last sheaf known as the 'clyack sheaf' was in by the end of September.

The seasonal round started once more interrupted now and again by a visit of the travelling steam mill to thresh the corn.

Unfortunately, I did not interview farming people in the 1970s when I spoke to people of the fishing villages. However, some farm-servants have written of their experiences in the first part of the twentieth century, and one farmer's wife, Mary Michie, wrote her autobiography, which includes part of the period. These sources have proved very useful in researching the past.

Married farm-workers lived in cottages belonging to the farmer and were referred to as 'cottars'. A single farm-servant – whether horseman, bailie, cattleman or orraman (odd job man, in other words) – lived in a room in the steading in the vicinity of the stable. In Aberdeenshire this room was known as the 'chaumer'. If such a worker had parents nearby and there was room for him in their house, he walked or cycled home each night.

Outwith Aberdeenshire, the 'chaumer' was called the 'bothy' and differed in its domestic arrangements as the men had to do their own cooking. In neighbouring Kincardine the bothy system was the one adopted for single men. As with the hierarchical observances of the chaumer men in the farm kitchen, in the bothy the highest in rank had first choice of seat and bed. He and his horses led the way out of the stable at the start of the day, and he was first to enter at the day's end.

That women too had to remember their rank comes through in Mary Michie's autobiography. When she started life as a cottar's wife in 1930, she had to go to the farmhouse to buy butter and get buttermilk to bake her scones. The farmer's daughter kept house for her father, and it transpired that she and Mary found much to talk about. They had their secondary school in common. Mary enjoyed her visits to the farmhouse and her conversations with the farmer's daughter. However, when Mary's husband found out about the visits, he immediately put a stop to them. Mary had forgotten that the farmer's daughter was the mistress while she was only the wife of a cottar.

The only time off work was every second Saturday and Sunday. This was when the single farm-servants and the kitchie deems bundled up their sheets and dirty clothes in a pillow case or cloth bag, and took them home to their mothers for washing. Those bundles in the bags, Mr Stephen explained, were called 'chackies', and were transported either by bicycle or on foot.

This scenario was to change radically as the century progressed. About 1900, the farms needed many men and many horses. Horses were required to pull the plough, the cart with the dung to fertilise the ploughed land, the harrows to prepare the earth for seed sown by hand, and after sowing, to cover the seed, and the rollers to make the land even.

When the climax of the year on the farm came in the form of harvest, the horses were, as always of immense importance. They pulled the reaper, and later, in the 1920s, the binder, described by Mr Mathers, a farmer who was interviewed, as 'the greatest invention in farming'. It cut down considerably on the harvest labour and the number of labourers required. Horses finished the job by carting home the harvested corn to the stack-yard.

Gradually, from about the 1940s and 1950s, tractors appeared on the scene. Mr Burnett told how, during the war, his father, who had had a two horse farm, bought his first tractor, a reconditioned one, which cost £150. Mr Mathers recalled his father buying a tractor at £150, but that he thought had happened in 1936. The days of the horse were numbered, and as they gradually disappeared many horsemen were made redundant. Some became tractor drivers. It was not long after this that the combine harvester was introduced, quickly followed by a series of machines for dealing with the straw that was left in the harvest field. Staff was drastically cut and the bothy system gradually died out.

While before the Second World War there were not many tractors, after the war most farms changed from horse power to tractor power. The movement from rural to urban areas where jobs were available in industry, and emigration overseas, which had started in the nineteenth century and affected Scotland as a whole, continued. Therefore not only were farmers welcoming to modern machines because they cut down on staff and wages, but there was also no great surfeit of labour to be drawn on, and many farmers really required the new machinery. That the farmers were able to afford to modernise so swiftly is explained by the fact that the farmers were more sure of a reasonable income than they had been before the war for there were now guaranteed prices for their produce and potato and milk marketing boards had been set up to look after their interests.

By 1950, there were few horses around. However, Mr Burnett spoke of horses still needed at the farm where he worked in the 1960s. Tractors could not get into the available space in the cattle court to clean it out. The horses were also still used to cart home turnips and the grain at harvest on this large farm. The end of horses was regretted by some farm-servants. They preferred their team to the noisy, smelly machine.

By 1990 larger, more competent, combine harvesters were on the scene accompanied by balers that made the straw into large rolls so tightly packed they were nearly completely impervious to rain. Still fewer men were now required. According to Charlie Allan, a recently retired farmer, many farms are now being run by one man. In one of his books he told how at harvest time his father had taken on workers till his work force was up to nine in all. Now, as he wrote, there was only himself and contracting firms that could be hired to come with their machines when required.

Haymaking too went through a period of change. In 1900 hay was first cut by scythe, a method superseded by horse-drawn mowing machines. Having been spread out and turned several times, it became dry enough to rake into coles. This was done with hand rakes till rakes pulled by horses were invented.

The 1950s brought new implements for the tractors – like hay balers which packed the hay into tied up rectangular blocks. By 1990 there were mowers, hay turners and balers that, as with the corn straw, turned out tight, round bales of hay. By this time many farmers were making silage instead of hay. This was in some ways easier for the grass did not have to be left to dry, and therefore the weather was not as important as it was when making hay.

Even the ways of keeping livestock went through radical change. At the beginning of the twentieth century hens were free ranging, laying eggs wherever the fancy took them. Halfway through the century they were being kept in deep litter sheds in which electric light fooled them into keeping longer days and instead of going to roost when darkness fell, continued to lay eggs. This proved to be a profitable method.

About the 1970s the battery method arrived which meant that each hen was confined to a cage, and had nothing to do but eat, drink and lay eggs. Many people disapproved of this method. It seemingly produced more eggs than ever, but shortened the lives of the birds. However, this practice appears to have gone out of fashion, perhaps, in part, because of consumer pressure.

There was usually a pig kept on the farm. Then, in the 1970s pig arks could be seen set about over a considerable extent of fields. Pig rearing had become big business.

For generations every farm also kept at least one milking cow for the household's requirements, and in the winter the cattle kept for the beef market were tied up in stalls in the byre. But starting in the 1950s the cattle were kept loose in cattle courts. No longer did food have to be served to separate stalls, and consequently the work force could be decreased.

The coming of BSE and salmonella in the 1990s made many farmers change completely from animal to arable farming. A European grain mountain was the result and the government started its 'set aside' policy whereby farmers are paid an amount if they allow a certain proportion of their fields to lie fallow. Many farmers resent this arrangement. They believe their job is to produce food and not to allow land, carefully cultivated by past generations, to lie unused.

In 1980, the government decided on a quota to control the amount of potatoes to be produced. Farmer, crofter and cottar had all cultivated potatoes, usually enough to be able to sell some. This had continued through the century, though the methods of harvesting potatoes changed radically. Up to and through the 1950s and 1960s school children on their 'tattie' holidays from school were depended on to bring in the potato harvest each October. In the 1970s machines appeared which made the gatherers' task easier. New diggers were soon followed by a machine called a potato harvester which needed only a few people to work with it. By the end of the century children had been superseded entirely by the harvesting machine.

The turnip crop too became less labour intensive. Mr Stephen explained that a sowing machine spaced out the seeds and meant that no longer was there a need to hoe by hand. A machine was also to hand to remove weeds from the turnip drills.

By this time there were not so many sheep to eat the turnips. Big farms in the early 1900s usually employed one or more shepherds to look after a large flock of sheep By the 1990s flocks tended to be small and the farmer himself acted as shepherd.

Mr Mathers claimed that 'mechanisation changed farming absolutely'. Undoubtedly, those fisherwomen of the past centuries would find our rural hinterland a far cry from the one they trudged through with their creels of fish.

CHAPTER EIGHT

Leisure in the Villages' Hinterland

Like the fishing communities, the farming communities held seasonal celebrations.

At the end of the nineteenth century, in some parts of rural Aberdeenshire, there was a festival called 'Beef, Brose and Bannock Day'. It started with the school children writing on the blackboard:

Beef, Brose and Bannock day, please let us home!
A' the folk in oor toon is ga'en tae Fogie Loan.

The 'toon' meant the 'farm toun' or group of people and buildings belonging to a good-sized farm. A holiday was always granted and in the farmhouses that evening the fare was beef, brose and bannocks.

In those days school holidays were decided upon locally. When the Clerk of the School Board thought his crops were ready to be harvested, he decreed that the children should start their 'Hairst Play' and school did not resume till the harvest had been gathered in.

The festival at end of harvest was known in Aberdeenshire as the 'Meal and Ale'. The womenfolk baked scones, cakes, oatcakes and prepared the meal and ale – a mixture of meal, stout and whisky. The barn was cleaned and decorated with greenery and the last sheaf of harvest, which was called the 'clyack sheaf'. The guests arrived and an evening of dance, song and poems followed, with music by fiddle, accordian and bagpipes.

Christmas, as in the fishing villages, was mostly ignored. Schools held parties for the children to which their relatives were invited to listen to the concert items performed by the pupils, and to provide tasty comestibles in addition to the contents of the paper bags containing mutton pies and buns. Games and dancing took place.

Mr Stephen told me that farm-workers were given the choice of Christmas Day or New Year Day off, and nearly always New Year was chosen. Children hung up their stockings on New Year's Eve – Hogmanay – and parish halls were decorated and dances held that night. They ended with the singing of 'Auld Lang Syne' followed at midnight with 'A Guid New Year tae Ane and A'.

Holidays were, in the past, given to school children on Fair days, and they spent their sixpences – a ha'penny at a time – on ice-cream, candy, sweets and swings. The principal business of the fairs was the buying and selling of horses and this reason of course disappeared with the mechanisation of farms. Aikey Fair was held in Aberdeenshire and lasted two days. There was one day of horse-dealing and then Sunday was the day for the usual stalls and fair ground rides and sideshows. Before it died out, it consisted entirely of the latter. Mrs Mathers remembered when bus-loads of people came from as far away as Glasgow to take part in the Aikey Fair amusements. This was she thought because at that time – the post second war years – amusements on a Sunday were rarely available. Before the First World War, Aulton Market was held every November in Aberdeen itself. There, five hundred to one thousand horses would be sold, and the farming people tried games of chance and bought gingerbread and handfuls of chipped apples costing a penny a handful while fiddles and bagpipes played, and some of them blustered about drunkenly, harangued by a crazy evangelist.

Other gatherings of farming folk were at the annual Games and Shows. Those meetings take place up to the present day.

The Games take place in a field in which various marquees are erected. John R. Allan described the events in the 1950s:

Sprinters sprint; slow bicyclists totter on the active side of inertia; girl dancers, hideously dressed in kilts and velvet and hung with little silver medals, posture and pirouette to a monotonous highland noise from the bagpipes. Huge muscled men toss hammer and caber.

The day ended with a dance in a marquee. Mr Stephen, who judges Tug o' War contests at Games, told me that at most Games nowadays the final dance has had to be abandoned because, on some occasions, young hooligans had arrived with knives and cut the marquee which the organising committees could not afford to replace.

Shows resemble games in many ways, but instead of competing athletes holding the stage, farm animals take pride of place, and are judged and win rosettes and silver trophies. There are on such occasions crafts tents and flower tents where farming people compete with each other to find out whose knitting, sewing, embroidery and other handicrafts are good enough to win prizes, and who has succeeded in growing the finest flowers and vegetables.

Other competitive occasions were the Ploughing Matches for which the horses were spruced up, fitted with highly burnished harness, decorated and be-ribboned. At the field to be ploughed, the horses and their harness were judged first, and then the ploughman's skill was put to the test. Mr Mathers remembered refreshments being served to the competitors of the match in the barn loft at his home, followed by the presentation of prizes by his mother.

Mr Mathers had no memory of any refreshments being provided at the hoeing matches. Prizes were presented to the most skilful competitors with the hoe. There was no dance after ploughing or hoeing matches in Aberdeenshire in the experience of the farmers I spoke to. Nowadays, the ploughing is done by tractor, not by horses dressed up in all their finery, and with the coming of machines that plant turnip seed neatly spaced out, and others that remove weeds from turnip drills, the hoeing match has become an event of the past.

There were, however, social occasions free of competition. Mr Mathers and Mr Burnett had each attended dancing classes in their youth for dancing was a necessary accomplishment in their society. In both cases the lessons had taken place in the barns on their respective fathers' farms. The music at Mr Mathers' class was provided by a pianist. In some of the country districts, dancing teachers came and taught the Eightsome Reel, Lancers, Quadrilles, Strip the Willow, Flooers o' Edinburgh, the Highland Schottische, Foxtrot, Quickstep, Waltz and others. Mr Mathers and his brothers attended local balls for which formal evening wear was worn.

Another interest of the Mathers brothers was amateur dramatics and they were members of drama clubs in the area. Mr Mathers had taken part in some of the favourite plays performed in the North East area. One he recalled was *Beneath the Wee Red Lums* by Joe Corrie, a very popular playwright in those parts in the past.

Competition came into this pastime in the form of Drama Festivals, which were in full swing in the 1950s. Drama clubs competed and received adjudications from professional actors. Those events still take place in the North East region. Every year the Buchan Heritage Society holds a drama competition for plays in Doric, the local dialect of the North East. The pages of *Heirskip,* the Buchan Heritage Society's annual magazine have been, since the Society's inception in 1984, full of songs, poems and stories in Doric, some by past writers, many by farming and fishing people of the present day. Very important in the Society's calendar is the yearly festival in the village of Strichen, Aberdeenshire.

North East people were, and are, also interested in music of various kinds. Lady Aberdeen of Haddo House, Aberdeenshire, a trained musician of professional standard, formed a choral society of the people of the district in the 1950s. Haddo Choral Society started with carols and Gilbert and Sullivan operas, but Lady Aberdeen set herself high goals for her choir, and moved them on to performing Bach's *St Matthew Passion* with the help of professional singers. According to John R. Allan, who wrote about this in 1952, the Bach performance was a great success. Haddo Choral Society still gives concerts.

At the opposite end of the social scale, and in earlier times, the lads in the 'chaumers' and 'bothies' composed and sang Bothy Ballads. John R. Allan sums up excellently the functions and contents of these ballads.

They express the whole life of the farm-servant – the ecstasies of love, the miseries of marriage, the meanness of masters, the greed of mistresses and above all the pride in the plough. Some of them reach the height of Rabelaisian humour, others sound great depths of bathos, but many are true and lovely songs.

An example he gives is:

> Braid up your gouden hair,
> Pretty Peggy my dear,
> Braid up your gouden hair
> Pretty Peggy – o,
> Our captain's name was Shaw,
> But alas he wede awa,
> He died for the love of a lady o.

A sample of bothy ballads about the work on a farm is *Drumdelgie*. As he drove the men on from task to task, the grieve's (or foreman's) refrain was 'Hullo, my lads, ye'll nae be longer here'. They were hardly given enough time to sup their brose and had to slave on, 'Till ye could wring oor sark'. No wonder that the ballad singer leaves this farm as soon as he can, and ends with:

> So fare ye weel Drumdelgie
> I'll bid ye a' adieu
> An' I'll leave ye as I got ye,
> A maist unceevil crew.

Allan comments that the bothy ballads were fading away after the First World War, the start of which in 1914 Allan regarded as 'the sunset of a world of greater ease and personality, when paganism had an exquisite bloom of decay and old customs flowered in an Indian summer of tradition'.

The farming people do not seem to have had a series of celebrations prior to a wedding such as the fisherfolk of Boddam had had at the end of the nineteenth and the beginning of the twentieth centuries. As for the fisherfolk, the rural celebrations included a 'feet washin' or 'blackening'. Boot polish, black-lead for polishing stoves, black treacle and soot were used – all ingredients easily obtained in farm kitchens. In the account I found, no women were mentioned as taking part in the farming ritual. After the groom was covered in this concoction, his workmates and lads from other farms, who had come to take part, sang and danced to the music of melodeon and fiddle.

The ceremony itself was a quiet church service. For one farm-servant's marriage in 1932, the bride bought a shirt and tie for her bridegroom for the occasion.

As everywhere else, football is and has been a popular pastime in the North East. Farming boys and young men are among the enthusiasts. In 1930, when George Cheyne was a 17 year old farm-servant in the district around the village of Collieston, he used to play football on summer evenings with the holiday makers residing in the village for the season. When I asked Mr Stephen about what he'd done in his spare time he said:

> We always supported Aberdeen – the Dons football club and went to see them playing on a Saturday. Kick-off would have been at three in the afternoon. After the match we'd go to the Market and have something to eat and then home.

Mr Mathers' sport was bowling, and one of Mr Burnett's grieves was a keen golfer.

The cinema and theatre were also attended by young farm-workers. Mr Stephen recalled the singer Robert Wilson and the comedian Jack Radcliffe at the Tivoli Theatre, Aberdeen. David Toulmin, a farm-servant, was a most enthusiastic fan of the cinema. Up to 1929, he tells us, the entertainment was silent films accompanied by a pianist in one Peterhead cinema he frequented, and in another by a four-piece orchestra – piano, drums, fiddle and bass. In 1930 he saw silent films with captions. Those Toulmin did not care for, but when they were superseded by proper talking movies, his enjoyment was great.

Social interaction played a great part in the lives of farm workers, as John R. Allan shows in his list of the cultural activities in rural North-east Scotland in the 1950s:

> The dancing class on Monday; the pictures on Tuesday; the dramatic on Wednesday; the small-bores on Thursday; the concert in aid of on Friday; the dance in the hall on Saturday; and besides those the junior agricultural club, the women's guilds, the S.W.R.I., the British Legion, the Scouts,

Guides, Cubs and little Brown Owls, the Curlers' Ball, the Farmers' Ball, the ploughing matches, hoeing matches, the Burns' Supper, the choir, the youth club and all the private occasions at the bridge.

Many of those activities continue as leisure activities of farming folk, but really, as with the fishing community in our time of media influence and levelling out, the people of the farming community on the whole just live the same as everybody else.

Bibliography

Adams, David G., *Bothy Nichts and Days* (Edinburgh: John Donald Publishers), 1996

Aitken, Margaret, *Six Buchan Villages* (Peterhead: J.&M. Aitken), 1976

Alexander, William, *Northern Rural Life* (Aberdeenshire: Robin Callander), 1981

Allan, Charlie, *Farmer's Diary* Vols. 2–4 (Methlick, Aberdeenshire: Ardo Publishing House)

Allan, John R., *Farmer's Boy* (London: Longman Group), 1975

Anson, Peter F., *Fishing Boats and Fisher Folk on the East Coast of Scotland* (London: J.M. Dent and Sons Ltd), 1974

Birnie, Helen M. and Sheila M. Jessiman, *St Fergus Past and Present* (Crimond, Fraserburgh: St Fergus Community Press), 2000

Buchan Heritage Society, *'Heirskip'* (Aberdeenshire: 1985–1998)

Chapman, R.W., ed., *Johnson's Journey to the Western Islands of Scotland* and *Boswell's Journal of a Tour to the Hebrides with Samuel Johnson L.L.D.* (Oxford: Oxford University Press), 1970

Cheyne, George, *All Muck and Clydesdales* (Fyvie, Scotland: New Concept Publishing), 1994

Cruden Bay Guide Book, 1908

Cruden Harbour Order

Dalgarno, James, *From the Brig o' Balgownie to Bullers o' Buchan* (Collieston, Aberdeenshire: Caledonian Books), 1986

Daviot, Gordon, *Claverhouse* (London: Collins), 1937

Devine, T.M., *The Scottish Nation 1700-2000* (London: Penguin Books Ltd), 1999

Fenton, Alexander, *Wird an' Work 'e Seasons Roon on an Aberdeenshire Farm.* (Edinburgh: The Mercat Press, 1992).

Fox, James, *White Mischief* (Middlesex, England: Penguin Books Ltd), 1984

Fraser, Dr James Fowler, *Dr Jimmy* (Aberdeen: Aberdeen University Press), 1980

Frazer, Sir James, *The Golden Bough* (Abridged edition) (London: Macmillan and Co., Ltd), 1932

Hamilton, Henry, ed., *The County of Aberdeen – The Third Statistical Account of Scotland* (Glasgow: Collins), 1961

Kemp, Willie, *Kerr's Cornkisters – Bothy Ballads* (Glasgow: James S. Kerr), 1946

Ludlam, H., *A Biography of Bram Stoker* (London: New English Library Ltd), 1977

Mackay, Adam, *Cruden and its Ministers* (Peterhead: printed by P. Scrogie Ltd), 1912

Mackay, Adam, *Distinguished Sons of Cruden* (Peterhead: printed by P. Scrogie Ltd), 1922

Macleod, Kathleen M., *On Aul Christmas Customs* and *Fisher Folk Wedding Customs, Transactions of the Buchan Club, (Buchan Field Club) 1963–1970* Vol. xviii Part II (Peterhead: Buchan Field Club)

Maple, Eric, *The Secret Lore of Plants and Flowers* (London: Robert Hale Ltd), 1980

Matthew, George, *Brose and Bogie Roll* (George Matthew, no place or date given)

Michie, Mary, *Cottar & Croft to Fermtoun* (Buchan, Aberdeenshire: Ardo House Publishing Company), 1995

Miller, James, *Salt in the Blood – Scotland's Fishing Communities Past and Present* (Edinburgh: Canongate Books Ltd), 1999

Ministers of the Respective Parishes, *The New Statistical Account of Aberdeenshire* (Edinburgh: Wm. Blackwood & Sons), 1843

Milne, James F., *T.E. Lawrence in Buchan* (Peterhead: J.F. Milne), 1954

Minutes of the Port Erroll Public Hall

Miscellany of The Spalding Club II (Aberdeen: The Spalding Club), 1842

Moncreiffe, Sir Iain of that Ilk, *Slains and the Errolls* (Peterhead: P. Scrogie Ltd), 1973

Pennant, Thomas, *A Tour of Scotland in 1769* (Perth: Melven Press), 1979

Pratt, John B., *Buchan* 1st edition (Turriff: Heritage Press, Scotland), 1978

Pratt, John B., *Jamie Fleeman* (Turriff: Heritage Press, Scotland), 1980

Scarlett Bernard, *Shipminder* (London: Pelham Books Ltd), 1971

Smith, Alexander ed., *A New History of Aberdeenshire Pts. I & II* (Aberdeen: Lewis Smith), 1875

Stoker, Bram, *Dracula* abridged by Nora Kramer (London: Scholastic Book Series), 1971

Stoker, Bram, ed. by Charles Osborne, *The Bram Stoker Bedside Companion* (London: Quartet Books Ltd), 1974

Stoker, Bram, *The Mystery of the Sea* (Stroud, Gloucestershire: Sutton Publishing Ltd), 1998

Toulmin, David, *Straw into Gold* (Aberdeen: Impulse Books), 1972

Toulmin, David, *Travels without a Donkey* (Aberdeen: Gourdas House), 1982

Turreff, Gavin, ed., *Turreff's Antiquarian Gleanings from Aberdeenshire Records* (Aberdeen: James Murray), 1871

Withrington, Donald J. and Ian R. Grant, General editors, Sir John Sinclair ed., *The Statistical Account of Aberdeenshire* (Wakefield, England: E.P. Publishing Ltd), 1982

Wood, Sydney, *The Shaping of Nineteenth Century Aberdeenshire* (Stevenage, Herts.: S.P.A. Books), 1985

Electronic Sources –

Video – *The Meal and Ale at East Letter Fairm* (Aberdeenshire: Carney & Lyall Productions Ltd), 1994

Boddam and District Community Council Webpages

Newspapers –

Peterhead Sentinel and Buchan Journal
The Press and Journal
The Aberdeen Journal